Policing
the Media

". . . society closes its doors, without pity, on two classes of men, those who attack it and those who guard it."

—Victor Hugo, *Les Miserables*

David D. Perlmutter

Policing
the Media

Street Cops and Public Perceptions of Law Enforcement

Sage Publications, Inc.
International Educational and Professional Publisher
Thousand Oaks ■ London ■ New Delhi

For information:

Sage Publications, Inc.
2455 Teller Road
Thousand Oaks, California 91320
E-mail: order@sagepub.com

Sage Publications Ltd.
6 Bonhill Street
London EC2A 4PU
United Kingdom

Sage Publications India Pvt. Ltd.
M-32 Market
Greater Kailash I
New Delhi 110 048 India

Printed in the United States of America

Library of Congress Cataloging-in-Publication Data

Perlmutter, David D., 1962–

Policing the media: Street cops and public perceptions of law
enforcement / by David D. Perlmutter.
    p. cm.
    Includes bibliographical references and index.
    ISBN 0-7619-1104-9 (cloth: alk. paper) – ISBN 0-7619-1105-7 (pbk:
alk. paper)
    1. Police–United States–Public opinion. 2. Police–United
States–Attitudes. 3. Police and mass media–United States. 4. Police
in mass media. 5. Cop shows–Social aspects–United States. 6. Saint
Louis Park (Minn.). Police Dept. I. Title.
    HV8138 .P45 2000
    363.2'0973–dc21   99-050428

00 01 02 03 04 05 06 7 6 5 4 3 2 1

Acquiring Editor: C. Terry Hendrix
Editorial Assistant: Anna Howland
Production Editor: Diana E. Axelsen
Editorial Assistant: Cindy Bear
Typesetter: Tina Hill
Cover Designer: Michelle Lee

Contents

Foreword

Ethnographers, scholars, and lay folk all see the world through a lens inflected by experience. Understanding the role and the relationship of the ethnographer to her or his subject provides data that are crucial for any ethnographic study. In its analysis of the way real people—cops—make sense of their visual symbolic environment in everyday life, *Policing the Media* provides an ethnography of police work that will be valuable for students, practitioners, and scholars in both criminology and communications.

I first became acquainted with David through letters of recommendation forwarded with his application to the doctoral program at the School of Journalism and Mass Communication at the University of Minnesota, where I had developed a curriculum in visual communication. *Policing the Media* got its start in my documentary photography class there. I routinely assigned each student the task of launching and (hopefully) completing a photographic documentary during a 10-week term. Considering my emphasis on thorough research and significant observation, the short time frame made for a difficult undertaking. I often met informally with students for an additional 10-week session so they could complete their projects. For his project, David chose to photograph the St. Louis Park Police. Rather than continuing for an extra 10 weeks, David pursued his subject for several years. He understood the ethnographic foundation upon which my documentary course was built, and he dedicated himself to honing his skills as an ethnographer in the research methods seminar I taught. He made it clear from the beginning that the limitations imposed by a 10-week term meant little to him, given his larger pre-defined goals.

David has produced a book that employs visual research methods to address important issues in visual communication. Instead of uncritically using pictures as interview prompts and exhibiting them as uncontested evidence, *Policing the Media* problematizes the role of the images used. But this is only one of David's accomplishments. In addition to his reflexive and thoughtful use of photographs, he takes the community as context and offers a concrete illustration of the interface between mass-mediated images and everyday life. He posits the relationship between popular representations of cops, public expectations of police behavior and policing activities, and officers' own presentation of self, on duty and off. *Policing the Media* presents ethnographic data that lead convincingly to the conclusion that representations *do* matter, and that media makers play an important role in shaping public consciousness through their manipulation of the symbolic environment.

Throughout my teaching career, I have tried to inculcate in my students an appreciation for the complexity of the photographer's endeavor and the responsibilities photographers have in representing the lives of others. David's work reflects these concerns. In addition, this volume embodies a blend of theory and practice and an interdisciplinary vision that is essential in our attempts to understanding others. I am honored to have been invited to introduce this volume, and I believe that the rich research tradition David inherits and advances will surely blossom as its descendants continue to enlarge its reach.

—Dona Schwartz
University of Minnesota

Preface

This book is concerned with (a) the interplay of mass media representations of law enforcement and crime and the work and beliefs of real-life police officers and (b) to what extent, how, and why real cops are in themselves mediators, that is, performers to the public and to themselves. The two questions are related because, as I will argue here, street cops perceive that the mass-mediated cop is in a sense a rival—one that has far greater influence on how we the citizenry define and appreciate police work. The focus of the book, then, is on the "social world" of media's impact, what Griswold (1994) defines as "the context in which culture is created and experienced" (p. xiv). The venue for the investigation was an ethnography I conducted from the winter of 1992 to the summer of 1995 of the St. Louis Park (SLP), Minnesota, police department. SLP is a border suburb of Minneapolis. In a relatively low-crime state—the legendary "Minnesota nice," as I can testify, does exist—the city's crime rate was about average. Its social geography is mixed: It has an industrial section, highways, family neighborhoods, and many small businesses. Its population during the day hits about 100,000 and at night falls to about half that number. In demographic makeup, SLP is predominantly white (90%) but with growing African American and immigrant populations; it also has the largest concentration of Jewish residents of any city in the state. In addition, there are several large senior living centers and nursing homes. Class distinctions are noticeable but in typical Midwest fashion not blatant, with areas ranging from wealthy neighborhoods with large, expensive family homes to moderate-income dwellings to poor sections (by suburban Minnesota standards) with low-income apartment buildings.

The SLP Police Department (SLP-PD) itself was small, comprising no more than 50 regular officers; a dozen sergeants, detectives, and lieutenants; one captain and one chief; and about 20 other staff, including dispatchers. All were and are based at a single station located only about 4 blocks from the apartment building in which I lived during that period. Only 4 to 6 regular officers patrolled the entire city at any one time (the official and thus unused term is *routine preventive patrol*). When my ethnography began, 2 officers were female; 2 more women were hired during my study. About 10 officers served for me as fully involved informants, those with whom I rode along most often. The PD administration knew of my study, approved it, and never put any restrictions on it save a tacit agreement that I would try (a) not to get killed and (b) not to obstruct officers in their duties.

Unusual for academic participant observation of cops (a term I use here as they do, without negative connotation), this study was partly a *visual* ethnography. With single-lens reflex camera in hand, I rode with cops, observed, listened to, talked with, and sometimes took black-and-white (or, more rarely, color) pictures of them. Often I watched silently, mostly when cops were interacting with the public. Other times, in long, long hours alone with a single officer in the squad car, I conversed. About halfway through the study, I joined their ranks—in a very restricted sense—by becoming a reserve police officer. I then rode along in uniform (powder-blue shirt rather than the cops' dark blue) but without a gun. Ironically, this change in status actually reduced opportunities for picture taking, as I became marginally more involved in assisting with police duties.

Because I first began the ethnography not as a reserve police officer but as a citizen and I carried a camera and took notes, it was instantly evident to the natives—the officers—that I was in some way studying them. Gary Allan Fine (1980) has suggested that ethnographers can adopt various levels of openness about their role: *Deep Cover, Shallow Cover,* and *Explicit Cover.* Deep cover is the undercover ethnography in which the researcher affects to be a natural participant in the environment and community. In explicit cover, the researcher reveals her or his role, intentions, and exactly how she or he plans to use the data. In shallow cover, a "middle ground," the researcher reveals general goals—for example, "writing about what you do"—but does not outline details of interests or intentions.

This last category describes my status with the police. I told them truthfully (both voluntarily and when asked), "Well, I'm interested in your work, what cops do on the street, talking about it and showing it." I used the material and photos gathered in the study for teaching and on occasion invited officers, department administrators, and other law enforcement personnel to address my classes. They were also aware that the work would be published someday in article or book form, although I assured them for the academic market, not the front page of the (despised) newspapers. I did not explicitly relate that I was particularly interested in their view of the interaction of mediated reality and their world. This was so often a manifest or latent topic of conversation with the officers that it seemed heavy-handed to emphasize its importance to me.

As a mass communication researcher, however, I was already interested in learning about a paradox of the street cop's role in a mass-mediated society. On one hand, our para-experience with police and the legal system is vast. Cops are familiar figures from literature, film, and especially televised fiction, news, and so-called "reality" shows. Crime (and crime fighting) is probably the single most common genre in both dramatic and nonfictional television and film (Ericson, Baranek, & Chan, 1987, 1989, 1991; Katz, 1987; Reiner, 1992, chap. 2; Schlesinger & Tumber, 1994; Sparks, 1992). Vicariously, all of us have viewed via the TV set or the movie screen cops chasing crooks through city streets, chain-drinking coffee during a stakeout, deciphering clues at a crime scene, or grilling a "perp" at the station. The scenes, dialogue, and poses of police work are clichéd. Moreover, as several cultural researchers have noted, much television programming in general and cop shows in particular use styles of cinematography and narrative that obscure the line between "reality based" and "fictional" (Cavender & Bond-Maupin, 1993; Linton, 1992). *NYPD Blue,* for example, uses documentary codes of realism that mimic the codes of news.

On the other hand, the world of the cop—the real cop—is secretive, a sort of guild, not open to easy dissection by the casual observer, especially through the limited personal experience most people have with police work. Our lived experience is generally minimal: For most of us, a speeding ticket or reporting a stolen stereo is the only authentic cop encounter. This was certainly my impression: I was a moderate viewer of news and fictional programming about law enforcement before I began my ethnography. Yet, a week into the study, a cop said to me, "This isn't like the crap they show on TV, is it?" Indeed, real-life law enforcement was not like what I saw on TV, and, in fact, it seemed not to lend itself to the bowdlerization that TV demands. Over 2 years, many illusions were shattered. For this reason, my own impressions as a member of the televisual audience of mass-mediated cops now encountering the real thing were and are part of the data for this study.

Questions arise from this situation. How do these two worlds coexist and collide? How do the mediated cops affect the beliefs and behaviors of actual, living police officers? What do real cops think about their two-dimensional screen cousins? What do real cops think are the influences of mass media on their "customers" (the public and the criminals)? These are essentially questions about how people negotiate the relevance and meaning of mass media imagery, symbols, primes, and narratives in their daily lives (Fine, 1977; Gamson, Crocteau, Hoynes, & Sasson, 1992).

Studying issues of mass media and society through an ethnography may seem inappropriate because field research necessarily examines limited communities. Yet, focusing on small audience groups, from *Dr. Who* fans to romance novel readers, has become an uncontroversial facet of media studies, whether by students of mass communication or others. Ethnography in general or participant observation in particular is one way to "get closer" to such audiences. Here, crucially, the audience studied (street cops) was also, indirectly, the *subject* of the mass media portrayals to which it responded. The added dimension of visual ethnography not only allowed the use of pictures as illustrations and tools of analysis but also prompted commentary and reaction by these subjects (see Schwartz, 1992). Finally, creating pictures of subjects that are already common in media portrayal, whether in prime-time dramas or cinema, can in itself be a reflective enterprise. The researcher begins to understand, not just by studying media texts but by creating them, the importance, power, and complexity of the codes, conventions, and clichés of the style, content, and connotations of those portrayals. As discussed later, sometimes when taking pictures I also felt weighed down by the dramatic and aesthetic standards of *Hawaii Five-O, Adam 12, Homicide: Life on the Street,* and *World's Toughest Cops.*

This book, then, is a limited report; its claims may or may not validly extend to other types of police in other regions, with larger or smaller forces, or serving different kinds of communities. Nevertheless, many of the findings match, support, or complement those uncovered through previous ethnographies and by other methods such as content analysis or surveys. For this reason, I also include a summary of previous research about the televisual world of crime and law enforcement, what cops think about it, and its possible effects on the public and cop work.

Yet simply reviewing the content of TV cop shows and then producing a checklist of divergences with the observed world of real cops is not in itself a satisfactory approach to the issues. Real cops do not refrain from attempting to mediate reality themselves. When they go on a call, they take into account public expectations. A textbook on policing sums up the situation as follows:

> Citizens have certain *expectations* about the police. These expectations are formed from a wide range of influences—for example, word of mouth, movies, promises of politicians, or "intuition." If the police meet a citizen's expectations, the person is more likely to have a favorable image of the police. Problems arise when these expectations are based upon unrealistic criteria. (Radelet & Carter, 1994, p. 205)

I add that cops believe that television is a major source of cop stereotypes, including many "unrealistic criteria" by which the public judges them and their work performance. Thus, although real cops distinguish between TV cops and themselves, they do not believe they live outside of a mass-mediated world. In addition, when in public they *perform,* not completely unlike the scripted and directed TV actor, in a way and style calculated to maximize audience impact.

The role of mass media here is worthy of study. What influences of mediated reality do we find in the daily routine and extraordinary events of cop work? More so than most "normal" people, police officers face situations that present intensely (and dangerously) ambiguous signs and causes. To maintain some level of cognitive cohesion, they must construct a kind of "interpretative framework to order fragmented experience" (Stewert & Sullivan, 1982). The suggestion that is developed here is that one interpretative framework cops employ is media-centric: *Cops feel that TV and movies are the standard to which other people hold them.* Relatedly, mass communication researchers have spoken of a third-person effect: People believe that others are more prone to be negatively influenced by mass media texts than themselves (Cohen & Davis, 1991; Cohen, Mutz, Price, & Gunther, 1988; Davison, 1983; Gunther, 1991). The cops studied in the ethnography believed (or acted as if they believed) that the public—including criminals, victims, and the press—was affected by mass-mediated representations of cop work. They know also that those expectations often cannot be met by their own actions and words. In this they do not necessarily perceive personal failing but rather a diminishing of autonomy and power. When combined with stories of "the way it used to be," when cops had greater freedom to prevent crime and enforce justice, the collision between mediated reality and street reality does cause noticeable effects on attitudes and behavior.

The book itself tries to encompass both the record of research on the televisual portrayal of police (i.e., the content of mass media) and the results and implications of the ethnographic study (i.e., the content of the "street"). The former comprises a *sine qua non* for evaluating the latter. Although ethnography, as will be elaborated later, adds to other research methods, it does not eclipse or obviate the need for them.

Accordingly, Chapter 1 deals with my experience of observing police officers and taking pictures of them. Such auto-observation is a useful entry to negotiating one's own understanding of the experience of ethnography. I describe how the process of making still photographs revealed something of the acculturation process of mass media; in turn, the cops' reactions to the picture taking and its products also served as examples of their general attitude toward mass media representations of their profession. Cops believe that people expect to see TV portrayals of police played out in real life, so they assumed that what I wanted was to find incidents in their work that displayed these norms and forms.

Performance for the camera, in real life, is not an ad hoc enterprise: It is part of the police officer's job. Chapter 2 outlines the conception of the dramaturgical metaphor and its application to street cops. It emphasizes that performance is a natural part of human action both through mediated forms of communication and in naturalistic settings.

Chapter 3 reviews studies of the content of television portrayals of crime and law enforcement. It also lists and discusses the basic contrasts between the mediated image of cops, what cops believe is the true description of the work life, and how the difference between the two may affect cop and public behavior when they interact.

Chapter 4 sums up major previous ethnographic research on cop work. In general, most studies argue for the cop's role to be full of inherent tensions and contradictions. These especially center on their dual role of "keeper of the peace and deliverer of justice" versus their officially sanctioned role as law enforcer.

In Chapter 5, I focus on the "front stage"—how cops deal with the public and how much of this constitutes a pre-scripted act—and the "back stage," where a different set of thoughts, actions, and behaviors are expressed, including "hidden transcripts" of complaint or criticism of the public, superiors, and other cops.

Chapter 6 questions the conception of "cop as outsider." To what extent do cops feel alienated from the very system they are sworn to enforce? How do they view mass media's role in the quality and quantity of that alienation? What is found is an ironic mimicry of television in which cops feel that they live in a Gerbnerian "mean world" consisting of a mendacious public and dangerous criminals.

Chapter 7 attempts to resolve some of the issues raised by the ethnography but also suggests some that, like many crimes, are not solvable. The main conclusion is that in searching for media influence on daily life, indirect influence based on assumptions of strong effects is an important factor. Real-life cops' beliefs about the power of media may drive what they do on the street; any attempts to build better police-community relations must recognize this fact.

A basic premise is that people's hopes and fears are affected by what they think they know, based on the evidence that they trust, arising from both the TV world and from what they have personally experienced. This is a human universal. In describing the anxiety and paranoia of the peasantry in the first year of the French Revolution in 1789, historian George Lefebvre (1973) commented,

> What matters in seeking an explanation of the Great Fear is not so much the actual truth as what the people thought the aristocracy could and would do; and it was not so much what happened as what the townspeople and peasants believed to have happened that stirred them into feverish activity. (p. xiii)

Likewise, what people believe to be true, no matter how fantastic or actual the basis of that belief, affects what they do and thus becomes a social fact, a segment of extramedia reality. In the *fata morgana* that often tempts researchers trying to prove definite causal relationships between media content and behavior, such perceptual maps are in themselves proof of the power of mass media in our lives. This is true for the police and the public and profoundly influences the system of law and justice in our country today.

In short, because so much of what is presented here deals with perception as well as observation, several concepts of projection and reality will be used. The term *street reality* refers to what happens in the cop's material-physical world. It is, of course, reality as assessed by the researcher and thus should be viewed as much a subjective approximation as any other reality. Nevertheless, it is, in a sense, a reference reality of what people (mostly the cops, the subject of the ethnography) think is the true nature of the population and events in their world. *Media(ted) reality* is the representation of the world of law enforcement found in mass media in general but on television in particular because this is the locus of most research on content and effects of cop and crime texts. These mental and corporeal worlds may converge or diverge, but all are important, and all may affect the beliefs and behaviors of cops (and others) on the street. In ethnography and in life, the mental map guides the actual journey.

AUTHOR'S NOTE

Gary Allan Fine (1993) has spoken of the "illusion of omniscience" of ethnographers who re-create "a scene with attendant bits of talk," thus implying to the reader that all that happened was heard, understood, and now is being faithfully reported. Furthermore, by employing the argot of the natives, we hint that we have mastered the *Sprachgefühl* of the insider. This is hardly a novel phenomenon: Ancient historians, rhetoricians, and biographers quite unashamedly invented entire speeches that they attributed to generals and emperors. Even the most honest among them, Thucydides (1928), admitted,

> As to the speeches that were made by different men, either when they were about to begin the [Peleponnesian] war or when they were already engaged therein, it has been difficult to recall with strict accuracy the words actually spoken, both for me as regards that which I myself heard, and for those who from various other sources have brought me reports. Therefore the speeches are given in the language in which, as it seemed to me, the several speakers would express, on the subjects under consideration, the sentiments most befitting the occasion, though at the same time I have adhered as closely as possible to the general sense of what was actually said. (p. xxii)

In the realm of fiction, W. Somerset Maugham similarly commented that he could not abide stories told in the first person that included transcripts of long conversations. How, he asked, could the reader suspend disbelief to credit the narrator with exact recollection of all that was said?

In this book, the quotes from police officers and others were reproduced from my own transcriptions. Even so, the statements are not verbatim because in taking notes I would often drop repetitious words, stutters, or nonword sounds. In other cases, I tried to jot down a paraphrase after the fact (signified here by the *"PP:"* notation and enclosed in quotes) of what an officer or a member of the public said. In such paraphrases, I attempted to capture the meaning, language, tone, and key words of the incident and the actor. The reader should keep in mind, however, that missing from any quote, whether faithful in word content and order, is a true feeling of context—what it was like to actually "be there." Moreover, another observer, with other research goals and expectations, might report a different scene that would be no more or less accurate.

Acknowledgments

All ethnographers should be grateful to the subjects of their work, but I owe a special debt to the officers of the St. Louis Park Police Department. They were not only guides and informants but also exemplars of how people can cope with stress, chaos, provocation, and danger and still emerge with humor and humanity intact. These are men and women who, for relatively little recompense and even less gratitude, risk their lives to serve and safeguard a citizenry with which they have no personal connection. No facts presented or conclusions drawn from this study should obscure that fact.

I thank Anne Jett, without whose help this book would never have been finished.

My wife, Christie, gave me invaluable assistance in preparing and critiquing the manuscript.

Dona Schwartz reviewed this manuscript, and her suggestions considerably improved and focused it.

Gina Dubrowski printed about half the photographs displayed here.

Gratitude is also extended to Randy Johnson, Bill Eilers, Joan Conners, Hannah Gourgey, and Ramona Lyons, who at one time or another responded either to a draft of this work or to some of the ideas contained therein.

Finally, I wish to note my appreciation to the patient and supportive editors and staff at Sage: Terry Hendrix, Kassie Gavrilis, Diana Axelsen, Anna Howland, and Gillian Dickens.

*   *   *

The completion of this manuscript was partly funded by a Lee Griffin Research Professorship.

Viewing and Picturing Cops

Because they are always on display, cops have a keen sense of image consciousness; keeping up the cop persona requires considerable mental, physical, and emotional energy. The need to be seen doing something—what on the contrasting medium of TV would be classified as "action"—forces them on occasion to behave outside the boundaries of experience-drawn logic and reason. One example taken from my ethnography: an early morning medical call. The officers arrive at an apartment before the paramedics. It is a crib death. A baby no more than a month old is, as the lead officer described, "cold, stiff, and blue." It has obviously been dead for most of the night. The parents are hysterical, as might be expected. They demand, *PP:* "Do something! Where are the paramedics?" The latter are on the way, but cops are almost always first there on "medicals" as well as crime calls. The parents expect the officer to jump in, to perform a miracle. The officer in question is one of the more stoic of the breed and, later speaking of it, he shrugged to me and said laconically, "I couldn't just stand there." So he gave this dead baby CPR until the paramedics arrived. He knew it was hopeless—not to mention a grisly experience. And the parents probably realized there was no chance of recovery as well. But he had to do it, or rather he felt he had to do it given the audience of the moment before him.

This is not a case of a performer playing to the follies or fashions of the audience, enunciating to the third balcony, or hamming it up for the admirers in the front row. Lived metaphors are much more serious business. I asked the officer if the parents blamed him because he could not resuscitate the infant. His reply, which took a few moments in coming, was that he did not know, but "I had to do something with them watching." He appeared disturbed by the episode so I did not pursue the line of inquiry, and we never brought it up again. What had the parents wanted from him? If, by some miracle, the baby had gasped to life, the

---

The notation *PP:* indicates that the following quote is the author's paraphrase. See Preface, p. xv.

cop would have been a hero. The resurrection unfulfilled, was he the scape-goat? The vague sense of not fully satisfying the audience can be both ignored and absorbed. Another officer commented on the incident: "On TV, cops have it clean. They save the kidnapped girl, slam the bad guy."

The question of what cops should and can look like, as well as who sets and maintains those standards, was obviously at the forefront of my study, the more so because it was intended to be also a visual ethnography. Taking pictures while studying a community, with the right application and results, assists the entry into the group (pictures as "can-opener"),[1] captures often complicated events that occur quickly (arresting multiple action), maps out the provenance of the work setting and communal environs (pictures showing details of place), and other assorted functions. But taking pictures can itself be a tool of reflection both on the act of picturing and on how such pictures are regarded by the audience, including the cops themselves.

It is important to begin this study, therefore, by reviewing the photographs this ethnography produced and outlining how they may suggest insights about the exigencies, both manifest and latent, of the cops' image. To do so, it is necessary to balance the points of view of two audiences for the images. The first is my own on the act of taking pictures of real cops. The second is that of the cops: my interpretations of their views of the photographs I produced. Crucially, whatever specific meanings that individuals or audiences encoded into or decoded from the pictures or from the process of making pictures, what made the pictures "good" in terms of style and substance were the inculcated norms and forms of the mass-mediated cop. By going inside to candidly express my reactions and trying to assess those of the cops, the discussion is opened.

LOOKING BACK THROUGH THE VIEWFINDER

One of the main claims of visual ethnography is that the pictures produced are part of the anthropological or sociological inquiry—less illustrations than thought-driven and provoking analyses of key moments in the lives of the subjects.[2] The sociologist with a camera should see "with theory," argues Howard Becker (1974) in one of the field's most influential essays. Douglas Harper, editor of *Visual Sociology,* has noted about his own teaching of the subject: "I have been repeating, like a mantra, that one should take a photograph with an idea in mind. The act of photographing includes a process of analysis" (Grady, 1996, p. 22; cf. Harper, 1990, p. 34). The resulting images are expected to differ from those constructed through other forms of visual media, including news and fictional drama. This is not to say that in isolation, the same photo that an ethnographer might produce would not also appear in a newsmagazine or as a still in a popular film. Rather, it is the way we claim to *use* those pictures that is our distinction.

The major element in that claim is that we do not make pictures to entertain or shock but to reveal and inform. The assertion that ethnography does not set out with the goal of producing entertaining images is both a political act and an attempt at group self-definition. No ethnographer wants to be confused with an avid, jostling news camera team seeking out the "money shot" of a high-action spot news story—norms of high kinetic content that have permeated almost every part of the culture (cf. Perlmutter, 1992, 1997, 1998). Neither do we want our audiences to mistake our imagery for that exhaustively produced by a multitudinous crew on a Hollywood back lot. That is not us, we say; that is not what we do. If some of our pictures fall along those lines, it is only to call attention to those very pictures in reflexive analysis of the modes of presentation in popular media; we mimic only to critique and understand. So research methods and ego validation concur as they do in the cop world or in any other profession or avocation. In rejecting the norms of "entertainment" as the goal of the images, we in essence dare to be dull in our subject matter, if not in our composition.

We can question, however, to what extent that dullness is defined. Entire ethnographic projects might consist of women making bread or chicken farmers feeding their flock, the layouts of corporate offices, or furniture in a suburban house. In any other setting besides the ethnographic meeting or journal, such images would be, in a word, shredder-fodder, the debris of the cutting-room floor. If used in any mass media program, fact or fiction, they would not be the main topic of the narrative but perhaps filler shots, cutaways, some ancillary element to the main focus on the development of plot, story, and action. In the hands of the ethnographer, the ordinary can be lifted into the fascinating, belying the myth that dullness should be the object (Schwartz, 1992). A film about cops, for example, may very well show a scene of the hero resentfully filling out a form or report. But report filing is only the precursor or segue to some other moment of higher voltage, gunplay, or demolition—no prime-time drama or cop movie has ever confined itself with the ways, means, and processes or personal, social, and group implications of the act of form filing. Crucially, we do not deem ethnographic pictures inconsequential; we agree they are important and revealing, the stuff our research is made of. The ethnographer has created a code of picture production whose products, if not always antithetical or deviant from those of most mass media, are used for purposes largely unexplored by (and uninteresting to) the mass media producer and image makers.

A picture such as the one presented in Figure 1.1 plays with such conventions. A young man—only 16—assaults his wife in plain view at the mall. The cops are called. He runs for it and is found at the National Guard recruiting station. *PP:* "He was asking about signing up. I guess he thought the Guard was like the Foreign Legion [where your crimes are excused in return for service]." Visually, I found the contrast—between the signs and symbols of national service and the fact that a young man was being handcuffed and arrested—to be striking. The recruiter (face obscured) is somewhat dour witnessing this unexpected event. The cardboard National Guardsman, rifle in hand, impassively observes the scene. And on the extreme left (unfortunately partly cut off) is a

Figure 1.1.

sign reading "Do the Right Thing." Other elements as well combine to display the absurdity of human behavior that cops often confront and the complexity of the world they patrol. Another officer comments about this picture, "Who knows why people do anything? It's not like on TV, where you find out everyone's motivations."

The ethnographer is also as embedded in the direct and indirect mass mediation of society as any member of other groups, including cops or lawbreakers. Part of the "ideas in mind" we have reveals the culture's influence on us as well as the ways we reveal the culture. We may be politically aware of the content and effects of codes of visual practice, but we still grew up with them. To deny that we are influenced by mass media in the same way as everyone else—whatever that way may be—is to privilege our status as omniscient sages. This is crucial to understanding how any of us sees cops—whether on a TV set, through a still camera's viewfinder, or from a passing car on the highway. We have watched innumerable murders on television; likewise, we have absorbed many scenes of jiggling bosoms, flexed abs, and casual sex from TV and movie screens. We too have sat back and let thousands of advertisements fill our brains with fantasies that if we buy this brand of Clamato juice, car, or blue jeans we will become more attractive, popular, or successful. Most important for this study, both I and my readers have watched countless hours of mediated cops and robbers. We live here in "TV land"; we do not just work here and check out at the end of the shift. Cops can enact some closure when they take off the uniform; people living in a mass-mediated society do not have the same luxury afforded by simply turning off the tube.

My ethnography recapitulated this ellipsis of modern life; it began about the time that the Rodney King video was first being shown nationally. It did not seem a very good context in which to call a police department and propose being allowed to take pictures of officers at work, with no restrictions and no end date. In fact, I had a certain pessimism about the endeavor, expecting to be turned down by many police departments before finding one that would allow me access. It was important, however, to try to conduct the ethnography in a department that served the same town in which I lived. The contrast between the neighborhood as viewed by my prior wholly civilian self and the cops' perspective through the windshield would only be schematized and eventually fleshed out in this way. Surprisingly, the captain of the department made his decision within days. I could ride along; I could take pictures. Our discussion of my role was rather vague, and he asked fewer questions than I expected. I think the fact that I was not a journalist but an academic suppressed some of the alarm bells that police officers must normally hear when they think they are encountering inquisitive members of the fourth estate. Perhaps, too, my agenda of learning about cops and using the pictures as a teaching and research tool, even if it did not make complete sense to them, at least was relatively innocuous compared to newsmagazine publication. One promise I did make, not as the price of my ethnography but as a courtesy stemming from it, was to show the police the pictures that I took.

This in itself was a research method. It constituted a form of photo-elicitation that sought out reactions in the subjects who revealed their own "spontaneous and emotional subjectivity" toward images of themselves (Faccioli & Harper, 1996, p. 4; cf. Gold, 1991; Harper, 1987). Indeed, they had much to react to. Throughout the ethnography, during my civilian period and my reserve period, I took thousands of pictures.[3] Pictures were "can-openers" to the subject (e.g., "Let me have one of those when you print them."). Essentially, the officers looked at my pictures of themselves and responded to me—while I was taking the photographs and afterwards—with comments, both about the content and form of the images and how they interpreted their meaning and estimated their representativeness. Most interesting, when talking about pictures still in my camera or about photographic prints laid out before them as prompts or as souvenirs, they also spoke of how they thought those pictures would be interpreted by others, the amorphous public who neither shared the experiences that produced the photographs nor understood police work through any mode other than mass-mediated representations of cops. The pictures, then, enabled me to learn about my subjects, but also through the pictures they were able to relate their own impressions of their image as distilled through photography, mass media, and the interplay of their purposive, front-stage impression management and the prejudices and a priori hopes, fears, and expectations of the community.

WANTING SOMETHING TO "HAPPEN"

Mass media's most important success in its infiltration of everyday life has been its ability to create standards for its own realism. For example, although most viewers have no experience with being in combat, a film that concentrates on the grisly forensics of battle and features hard-bitten, disillusioned, cynical soldiers is considered realistic (Perlmutter, 1994, 1999). Likewise, the cop show that presents hard-bitten, cynical, disillusioned cops fighting the system is purported (again a convention!) to be authentic. Thus, the fantastic defines the vicarious; what we believe to be real is actually what we think could or should be real. That most soldiers who serve in wartime never see combat and that most cops never fire their guns are realities that are literally not translatable into entertainment or "docu" media. This skewed normalcy was commented on by cops, both the inaccuracy of TV reality ("all they do is kill people and beat them up") and the relative discordance with their own situation ("you must think we do nothing for a living"). I felt I had a certain analytic awareness of the constructed nature of the mass-mediated representation of cops before entering into contact with officers at a real, although not necessarily representative, police department, but this awareness did not act as a prophylactic from my deviating toward a norm of expectation based largely on the mediated fantasy. In many ways, my own feeling, regardless of any actual procedure for the ethnography, confirmed cop suspicions about the public. I, too, tended to expect street reality to conform to televisual reality.

The element for which I found it most difficult to suppress a yearning was *action*. There was a constant tension within me about whether I was trying to shoot photographs that served the interests of the "ideas in mind" of my ethnography or those that, by the standards of fictional television or news photography, were "money shots" involving kinetic events. Action had many definitions: a car chase, which I was never involved in; pursuit of a suspect, which I followed only twice; a fight, which I witnessed three times; and gunfire, which I never saw. My thirst for action seemed to appear as an apotheosis in moments of torpor when nothing had happened for some time or was prompted by mundane events in the cop's shift that I called into contrast with the expectations that most people would have about police work.

An example of the latter arose in the circumstances behind the picture presented in Figure 1.2. It is a straightforward moment, a police officer and neighborhood children surveying hubcaps found abandoned on the street and then laid out for inspection on a lawn. The Found Property Report was filed in response, and the hubcaps were catalogued and taken into custody. The kids, squeaky-clean suburbanites, had found them by the side of the road. Who dropped them there? It is a mystery wrapped up in an enigma that does not beg a solution. I take the photograph, and I am pleased with the results: the kids, the hubcaps, the cop. Even though it is posed, it well displays the kind of work that the street cop finds more regularly in his shift than gunplay or car chases. It

Figure 1.2.

also illustrates the amiability of the encounter: an important and routine part of police work.

At the time, though, I wondered whether this was a picture worth taking. For anyone who creates visual images, action is incident. Was this worth my film, my time? Climbing back into the police car, the cop seemed to have similar questions about his own role. *PP:* "That should make *Cops*." We start joking about this, about an episode of a reality-based cop show in which every incident is mundane or where there are no incidents at all. Here, the nonincident enhanced my reflection, but—and this is a crucial "result" of my ethnography—the cop himself understood and appreciated the mediated norm of expectation for me and for him. My yearning for action was mirrored in his. I was not, in this sense, an outsider who had false delusions of police work whereas he was an insider who knew the truth and thus was set free from the prejudices of expectation that I held. To the contrary, in episodes such as this one, cops would often remark that this was "pretty dull stuff" or, sarcastically, "another action-packed adventure." Is there a contradiction here? The officers are "there," they know the reality that they live and work within. Do they think that the mundane is dysfunctional?

This question will not be answered so much as elaborated on later, but my reaction to their reaction, my mimesis of their expression of disappointment in the dullness of much of what they do, again underlined the constructed nature of our definition of reality. The cops shared my televisual culture, and so the indirectly mediated reality that they struggled with found similar manifest and latent eruptions in their discourse among themselves and to the ethnographer with whom they shared a police car. My own reaction was to some extent guilty. Did I have a right to feel bored? Ethnographers will admit in print, sometimes only many years later, that they fell in love with their subjects or, rarely, that they hated their subjects. But no researcher admits that the data he or she studies bore them stiff.

This was not the case here, I must emphasize. I was not bored with the subjects; rather, I shared their occasional boredom with what they did, especially when it was a trivial matter that probably could have been handled by someone other than a full-fledged, armed police officer. Sharing this sense of ennui to some extent helped dissipate it. It created another topic of conversation: Why are cops asked to do such things? So again, what may be a problem in an ethnography, even a visual one, may be exploited as a research opportunity, and a necessity may become a virtue. Talking about "dull stuff" revealed as much about the cop's world and his perceptions of its relationship to mass-mediated representations of police work as did moments of and discourse about action.

The other point when the dullness of the data became an issue was less an acute incident than a chronic condition. The high-speed chase was perhaps the premier event that in the years of my ethnography I never encountered and always wished for. This was, of course, not rational—pursuit driving is "the most dangerous weapon" that poses a considerable threat to everyone, including innocent bystanders (Alpert & Anderson, 1986; see also Alpert & Fridell, 1992). Yet it almost became a mental game with me each time an officer put on his lights and sirens to indicate that a car should pull over. Would the suspect speed off? Would this be the beginning of a chase? I looked forward to this prospect, and with two of the officers with whom I rode frequently it became an inside joke. Occasionally at car stops, I would say, "He's gonna go! He's gonna go!" One of the officers would quip that it was obviously my intimidating looks through the squad car windshield that prevented dangerous criminals, wanted on multiple felonies, from bolting. These comments were usually unleashed when we pulled up behind an older church lady type in a late-model Cadillac. In torpor, there may be strength or at least diversion. On long Minnesota nights in January, this is indispensable.

"HERE'S A GOOD SHOT"

Subjects of the visual ethnography's camera adopt one of four attitudes and physical deployments in relation to that of the camera.

1. *Director.* The subjects may pose directly for the camera, that is, prepare themselves in a stance, look, gesture, expression, or perhaps even dress that they intentionally wish to be imprinted on film as part of the record of the research or as a souvenir or a memento. They are fully aware of the camera and consciously act to stage and array what appears in front of it, including themselves. As Peter

Turner (1987, pp. 76-87; cf. Chalfen, 1987) has noted, such presented awareness is often a nervous reaction to the photographic act; being "on camera" is an invitation to do something—hence, the self-conscious mugging and "joky posing" of so much personal photography.

2. *Altered States.* The subject engages in some behaviors that are not directly constructed for photographic representation but is visibly aware that he or she is being photographed. This awareness may be directly communicated by looking at the camera every once in a while or altering behavior in some way to conform, again, to an estimation of what the appropriate visualization should be. Here the subject does not confront the camera and behave *toward* it but does behave with the camera in mind: The stiff movements and staccato verbalizations of bad amateur acting on video announce that "I'm on camera."

3. *Indifference.* The subjects know that a camera is present and could be focusing on them, but they continue their actions essentially unimpeded or unchallenged by this knowledge; that is, they "behave normally," as they would if no camera were present. A simple clue is that they do not look at the camera or freeze in front of it in self-conscious poses. Even so, in this state of interaction between ethnographer and subject, the former can never be quite sure of the true state of mind and its effect on speech and body of the latter. Subconscious mannerisms, gestures, and looks may have percolated into the subjects' performance so that the camera favors or ignores them.

4. *Obliviousness.* Finally, we have the rarest situation, when the subjects are completely unaware that they are being photographed. Perhaps it is a large, crowded room, a mass meeting. The photographer is in one corner. With a long lens or assuming a background stance, he or she can shoot while remaining unseen. In this situation, the photography may be covert.

The first three conditions predominated in my ethnography. At a minimum, cops knew that I was a photographer, that I was there with a camera, and that I could take pictures at any time. With officers with whom I rode along frequently, I had worked out largely unspoken arrangements that put some limitation on when and where I would take a photograph. Almost all of these restrictions involved interactions with the public—for example, not taking a picture that would provoke someone in a potentially violent situation. But I was willing to work within other boundaries as well. A sergeant asked me not to take any pictures of him during roll calls; his reason was simply that he did not like the way he came out on film. In the entire ethnography, only a handful of times was I specifically told by an officer not to take a picture at a given moment. More interesting, the phenomenon of looking at the camera that is the bane of photojournalists rarely occurred in the study. The reason this was so—why while looking through the viewfinder I did not often see a police officer staring bug-eyed at my lens—was partly a confirmation of their getting accustomed to my being around. My ethnography was, after all, held over the course of 2 years.

But another explanation delineates the main considerations of a police officer when engaged in interactions with the public. Simply put, a cop at the scene
of an incident is focusing on his or her duties. Because I was worried that my
presence might interfere with their work, I was constantly checking whether
they were going to make any motion to me to back off or stay away. Again, this
rarely happened. As the ethnography proceeded, it became clear that the cops
had other, more pressing concerns. It suggests a truism of visual ethnography:
It may seem incredible to those who have never practiced it that anyone from
South Sea islanders to suburban cops would get used to a stranger following
them around with a camera, but this is in fact what occurs. Although I never dis-
appeared off their radar screen, so that they were completely unaware that a
camera was present, neither did I see evidence of their changing their routine.

Critically, however, that the cops did not directly process my presence as a
reason to act differently does not mean that the behavior of the officers was
"natural." To some extent, the officer in public is always "on." Whether they
considered me a civilian, an intruder, or a true member of the fraternity and
sorority of cops was less important than that when I viewed them in public,
there were other viewers as well, from suspected criminals to victims or witnesses of crimes to other civilians offering help or in need of help. So the photographs I produced of cops in public settings can be said to be mediated by the
imperatives of impression management. Cops perform to the public; I photographed that performance. Photographs taken behind the scenes—what will be
discussed in the next chapter as Erving Goffman's (1959) "back stage"—are
another matter. These did contain behaviors that cops normally would eschew
on the "front stage": sitting around and reading a magazine, mock fighting with
other cops, and so on. Here, the ethnographer can only guess or infer to what
extent such behaviors were another form of act, another performance, perhaps
for themselves as much as those around them.

An interesting and, from the point of view of photographic production,
helpful development in the ethnography was that some of the cops actively
assisted in my picture taking, through encouragement, by providing opportunities or setups or actual direction. In fact, to understand cops' attitudes to
mediated production of imagery about themselves, this phenomenon, the
encouragement of picture taking, was more meaningful than the much rarer
discouragement. In the photograph in Figure 1.3, officers try to restrain and
simultaneously bandage the wrists of a woman who had (we were told on
arrival) attempted suicide with a straight razor. Taken early in my ethnography—only the second or third time I rode along with the officer I was with that
day—it is an example of a picture that I probably would never have taken if not
prompted to do so. When we arrived at the scene, I hung back outside the door.
We had heard it was a suicide attempt, and I thought a photographer would not
be a welcome inclusion to the scene that must follow. Later on, I would learn to
simply put my camera aside or let it hang unobtrusively, but at this moment I

Figure 1.3.

stood outside while the cops scrambled in. There were three or four other squads (i.e., squad cars) parked outside, their officers already in the apartment.

A few seconds later, my ride-along officer stuck his head out the door and said, "Come on!" I followed him in. There was the scene, more or less what you see in the photograph. The other officers were going about their business, not paying attention to me. The woman's head was turned away. A neighbor was watching the struggle; so was the victim's husband. I hoped nobody would mind if I snapped some photos, so I knelt down and shot away. Later, I went into the bathroom where another officer had told me the razor was and took a picture of the still life within the basin (see Figure 1.4). The woman was bundled up by the paramedics and transported down to an ambulance while the officers began to disperse. No one even commented on the picture taking. Back in the squad, my officer nodded his head as he gunned the engine. *PP:* "I got you some good stuff there, didn't I?"

The "good stuff," then and later, was action. This officer turned out to be the visual analog of the key informant in standard ethnographies, the person who opens doors for the ethnographer and acts as an adviser, introducer, and, to some extent, protector. There were five or six cops who I felt played this role for me in different ways. This particular cop, however, not only never interfered with my picture taking or second-guessed it, but he also actively suggested that I go ahead and take photographs in situations in which, for various

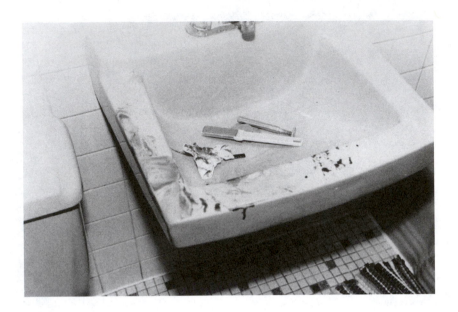

Figure 1.4.

reasons, most often being his safety and the stability of the scene, I would not otherwise have pressed my shutter and engaged my flash. This was repeated on several occasions: "Dave, this is gonna be good. You want your camera to be ready here," or "This guy's a live one. Better get ready." What was interesting about him was that he did not manifest any more noticeable awareness of the camera. He was not one of the subjects who too often stared back at me. He was just simply good-natured, an enabler. I saw that nature in his work and his attitude toward me. Once, during a house search, I ended up facing him in a room and without thinking flashed him head-on from about 2 feet away. This occurred in the twilight of a darkened house, with my strobe at F8, just as he walked forward, gun drawn, not knowing what to expect. He blinked and froze, then smiled and said, "Well, you got me there, Dave," and went on with his search, no doubt half-blinded. His support of my work did not seem to affect his own performance.

His attitude was the most forthright of any of the cops, but others as well, indirectly or somewhat less eagerly, enabled my picture taking. In every case, it is important to underscore, the pictures that they felt I wanted to take, that they assumed were the goal of my study, were those very pictures that reflect the stereotype of police work as violence and action. They assumed that I was looking to re-create, with my camera, the mass media representations that beguiled them, troubled them, and, they assumed, had largely duped the public, making their job more difficult. Examples include the following: *PP:* "I think that kid's gonna run for it; is your camera ready?" "You might wanna take your camera with you in here; this guy's gonna go." "Go ahead and take pictures, even if he fights." In most cases, however, the officers made indirect allusions to the kinetic potential of a scene. Sometimes they would look at my camera and say, "Okay, let's do it." Or, after an incident had played out, they would comment, "Too bad nothing happened there for you." So, for the officers that I rode with most frequently, the target of this enabling, the action pic, was their preferred suggestion for my view of their work.

Their assumptions of what I wanted, their value standards of what was good photography of them, were also revealed in an incident near the end of my ethnography. I brought several albums of all the pictures that I had printed into the department's file room, an area in which most of the forms are kept and where officers will often sit to wade through their paperwork. I wanted to give them a chance to leaf through my photos, make comments, and request prints of their own. Overwhelmingly, their preferences, the pictures that they stopped to comment on and to ask for copies of, were action pictures: cops with guns raised, cops running, struggles with suspects, moments of anger on the street. Pictures displaying the procedural aspects of police work were flipped past without comment.

In the field as well, the more mundane parts of police work were seen as unworthy material for my camera, not in terms of censorship but in terms of assumed lack of audience interest. "Jeez, who wants to see us filling out papers?" Such beliefs were expressed by the same officers with whom, over long stretches of time in the squad, I had the chance to talk the most about the discordance between the image of the TV cop and their daily lives, between mediated reality and street reality. This was not a case of cognitive dissonance. They did not maintain that the mediated cop was a nefarious influence and at the same time think that my camera should reproduce the media representations to make them look good because they thought that *was* good. Rather, they assumed that the value standard of judging police work was the one that people absorbed through mass media; hence, whatever audience I had for my pictures would seek that out also.

But it is not purely a case of cops thinking that they must look as people wanted them to look. They themselves—as evidenced by their comments and by other research discussed later—have a love-hate relationship of a sort with their televisual and cinematic counterpart. They resent having to live up to him or her, but they have absorbed the value standard of the definition of cop herohood. This was reflected, as previously mentioned, in the "keeper pictures," those the officers wanted prints of. One put it this way, asking me for a copy of a picture I had taken of him wrestling a recalcitrant violent drunk to the ground: "That's the one I think my kid would like to see, not me reading a newspaper during lunch." Hence, the influences of indirectly mediated reality bounce back and forth in the echo chamber of culture and society.

According to my records, at least three fourths of the keepers were action photos. The second most requested category was action *poses*. Here, a cop might, for example, ask me to take a couple of pictures of him at the shooting range firing his gun. I would in such cases try to stand in front of him, perhaps at a low angle, to enhance his look of power and force. Another frequent pose was by the police car or at the doors of the station. Finally, there were the "buddy shots" (e.g., "Hey, will you take a picture of me and Joe?"). Such poses, again, were a small minority of the photographs that the cops expressed an interest in having for themselves. Generally, they preferred natural events as the subjects of keepers; after an incident that I photographed, they might ask, "Do you think I could get a copy of that?" This was by no means a frequent or habitual occurrence. I never found a pattern of when they would or would not want a print. Sometimes they would comment on how an incident produced a great photograph—"greatness" denoted by its kinetic content—yet although that photograph included them, they would not ask for a print. Requests for prints were never insistent; they were asides. When, because of my sluggish printing schedule, I would give them pictures weeks or perhaps months later, they showed no sign of irritation or impatience. A picture was only interesting, not a monumental achievement on my part or theirs. I offer this as evidence that the cops did not create actions simply so that I could take pictures of them for their own ego validation.

"THEY'LL THINK WE'RE BORING"

People watching cops on television are not unaware that the officers file forms and sit around and that there may be a lull between calls. The time expended on such activities on television, however, is minimal. Cops may be shown having lunch, but a 45-minute extended sequence of a police officer munching his sandwich, sipping a Coke, and reading the newspaper has yet to appear in prime time. It would be novel and, perhaps for a minute or two, like films such as Andy Warhol's *Empire,* call attention to the strangeness of watching real-time exposition on film. But that novelty would wear off, and we can be assured that by the end of the presentation of the realistic period in the work life of a real cop, the entire audience would have sought out more scintillating drama, such as *This Old House* or *Bass Masters*. As we have seen, in this ethnography, a consistent finding was that the police perceived that the public had a stereotype of their lives being full of action, that the ethnographer carried this acculturated stereotype with him or her and that it affected his or her attitude toward the events and the act of taking pictures of cops, and finally and most important, that the cops themselves, although they were grounded in their own experience, still retained this and some of the value standards of media representations of cops.

If action seemed to be the common currency of cops and their audience, then the opposite, dull and ordinary incidents or time, was self-consciously viewed

Figure 1.5.

as somewhat of an embarrassment. In a word, the cops had the same standards of being bored as everyone else does, perhaps more acutely so because, unlike accounting, for example, it is generally assumed that their profession is consistently exciting. These sentiments were expressed directly to the ethnographer. In the photograph in Figure 1.5, an officer, a lieutenant, and a sergeant wait to testify on an assault case at the criminal court building in Minneapolis. We bided time for $2\frac{1}{2}$ hours in this room; I could have taken many pictures such as this one. Eventually, a secretary came to tell us that the case was postponed, and no testimony was given that day. It was a metaphor for the contest between the TV world and real world. In television, the representation of the passage of a long time in a static situation is accomplished by several techniques, from the spinning of hands in a clock face to the passing of the sun to the cutaway of a growing pile of pizza crusts or coffee cups of officers on stakeout. In real time, however, only real time is available. During the wait in the courthouse, the officers made several comments each, especially when I took a photograph, along the lines of, *PP:* "They're gonna think we just sit around and do nothing," or "It's a pretty dull picture, Dave; why are you taking it?" In short, they were conscious that the image of a police officer sitting in a waiting room twiddling his thumbs hardly fit into the expectations of the public. On an episode of *Law & Order,* the cut or fade would be not to the $2\frac{1}{2}$ hours in the waiting room but to the officer on the stand giving testimony. Although the actual event might confirm cynicism about the "suits" who control the system, it also, in the cops' view (perhaps quite legitimate), failed to "make them look good."

This was perhaps the greatest irony of the ethnography. Only a handful of times did an officer ever directly tell me not to take a picture in a potentially violent or dangerous situation. On the other hand, officers frequently expressed reactions ranging from surprise to mild irritation when I took pictures of them "doing nothing." These comments were so frequent that any self-censorship that occurred in the ethnography was precisely in the realm of suppressing in number, if not in type, pictures of officers engaged in non-stereotypical activities. Again, the ethnographer, consciously or not, may act to perpetuate the stereotype that she or he seeks to analyze and to some extent deflate. And, most revealing of all, no cop ever asked for a keeper of him or her filling out a report.

No matter that doing "nothing" was actually something important indeed. Waiting in court to testify, driving around on patrol, having lunch, sitting at roll call, filing a report, talking to another officer while parked in squads, walking around the mall, checking a back alley, putting on the uniform, cleaning the weapons, scanning computer databases, taking information from suspects or victims, chatting with merchants or local kids, prepping the squad car, and making sure all the equipment is in working order: These are all activities of which we may have glimpses on prime time, but they are never accorded the length and commonalty they hold in real life, nor does real life allow such events to always conspire to propel a central narrative. But they are all necessary. Cops must do them, if not technically to fight crime then to be ready to do so. Even a chat between cops on a slow afternoon about fixing a patio deck on a lakeside cabin is functional to police work. It builds camaraderie and enhances the ease of working together. Such downtime is also necessary to prevent the cop from being a nervous wreck: One cannot be "on," active, and kicking down doors for an entire shift. Indeed, in terms of preventing crime, keeping the peace, and enforcing the law, the dull and mundane activities of the police officer are in the end far more useful to the public than the action-packed and thrilling activities.

Cops know these facts of work life. Yet, they understand that filling the squad car with gas, however necessary and functional an activity, does not quite fit in, not only with the perceived expectations of thrills and spills that the public holds but also their own internalized value standards (see Figure 1.6). "Maybe I should have my gun out when I'm doing this," a cop commented. "It would add something to the picture."

These feelings of wanting to match the exterior stereotype of police work were, I felt, sensed by cops themselves; that is, they were both internalized and projected. They were internalized in that cops were well aware that on television, police are men of action; they also knew that an entire 8 hours on patrol, punctuated by a single car stop for a broken taillight and two barking dog calls, in no way matched this image. It was dull; they knew it was dull. I heard many times, "Well, this is dead. I wish something would happen," even though a happening may be an invitation to danger. This situation parallels that of the

Figure 1.6.

soldier who may prefer at times the kinesis of combat to the tedium of the rear echelon. But certainly as well, the consciousness of the discordance is a projection. Cops know that others—the public, including myself—have similar standards of boredom.

The ride-along is where these issues most came to the fore: It is the nexus at which people can really experience the cop's life, albeit briefly. It also affords cops an opportunity to show people what they do. I came under the impression that the ride-along—in which a civilian or a reserve officer accompanies cops on patrol—is a situation in which police feel some self-consciousness about the relationship to what they do and the image of what they do compared to the standard of the mediated reality of police work. One cop told me about his experience with an Explorer (police junior auxiliary younger than age 17 with a uniform much like that of the reserves). This particular girl rode along with the officer many times, and, as he put it, "We used to joke that she was a curse on crime. Every night that she would ride would be a dead night." The girl expressed especially the wish to be involved in some sort of chase, but that did not happen either. The officer described, with humor and irony, that the very last night before the girl left the Explorers and went off to college, he dropped her at the station where her car was parked and at that moment got a call that a chase was going on nearby; he peeled out in lights and sirens. He recalled the look of extreme disappointment on her face. His own feeling was less intense but nevertheless shared; he said he wished he had seen more action when she was riding along.

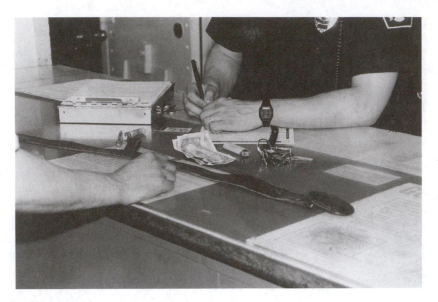

Figure 1.7.

Cops themselves cope with dullness in several ways, for it is not a concern only when others are present. Foremost, during much of the period when an outsider might see inactivity, they are actually performing important functions: The forms must be filed, for example. "Dave, I gotta say, I hope we have a slow night 'cause I got a ton of paperwork." Or, "Dave, you might wanna ride with someone else because I'm just gonna be filing, catching up." This is a balancing of the notion of drama. As mentioned earlier, it is the cops' perception that media heavily influence the view of what a cop does. Their qualitative perception of the content of media is little different than more formal analyses of programs dealing with law enforcement and criminality. However, they adhere to a strong effects school. In this chain of logic, it is natural for them to be sensitive about how what they are doing does not fit into the stereotype, even when they reject the stereotype.

Hence the reticence about the public display of the mundane. Yet, the idea in mind was important to me: the minutiae of procedure, how a police officer must catalogue everything he or she does (see Figure 1.7). The public, when confronted with the forms and filing, often rebels (e.g., "Why do you have to know this?"). But one way police maintain control over their environment, but in which they are also controlled, is in the following of bureaucratic procedure. A suspect must turn over the contents of his pockets and his belt in the booking room. The shoes must be released also; they will be put in a drawer, everything else in a manila envelope. It is an important ritual, one that reduces risk for everyone involved.

Figure 1.8.

Or paperwork (see Figure 1.8). One of the stereotypes of television that will
be listed later is the "supermodern lab" that answers all questions. A cop put it
this way: "On TV, they just call Smitty down in the lab and they get all their
questions answered. In real life, big-city cops, small-city cops: All of us have
to do a lot of our own work. Even detectives don't have a squad of flunkies." So,
for example, unknown drugs found on a suspect must be looked up; are they
illegal without a prescription? If so, were they stolen? What are their effects?
The narrative of the arrest requires such information; the cop discovers it for
himself or herself. To me, the idea in mind is the work concentration as well as
the autonomy and ingenuity of individual police officers—that despite a lot of
the controls that bureaucratic organizations try to put on them, much of the job
calls for improvising and overcoming, even when the targets of these efforts
are producing bureaucratic forms. Still, the officer asks me, *PP:* "Why take my
picture doing paperwork?" It's a mass-mediated world, after all; we just work
here.

NOTES

1. "The spontaneous invitation to the fieldworker to show his pictures is the result of a
unique function of the camera in many kinds of studies. Informally we can call this function of photograph a 'can-opener' " (Collier & Collier, 1986, p. 23).

2. Visual ethnographer Douglas Harper (1987) has explained that he chose the pictures to accompany an essay on the life of tramps not as "illustration" but to "represent

typical moments in the routine of tramp life" (p. 7). Harold Becker (1995), in assessing Harper's work, concurred that the photographs appear "not as illustrations, the way photographs appear in sociology textbooks, but as elements integral to the sociological investigation and therefore to a reader's sociological understanding. They contain, and express, ideas that are sociological in their origin and use, and thus may not be as transparent to an immediate reading as other photographs" (p. 11).

3. I did not show every photo to every officer. In fact, I never really developed a system of distributing copies of photos, which in any case would have been too expensive. The more haphazard system of giving photos to the officers every once in a while, taking pictures they wanted me to take and in a few cases letting some officers look through my scrapbook, seemed to work better for the more informal arrangement of the ride-along.

All the Street's a Stage

The driving force in the descriptions and analysis presented here arose from the perception that police on the street play out a role not unlike that of an actor in a theatrical performance. Such a dramaturgical metaphor is not meant to slight police work. Rather, it allows the observer to note how cops, their superiors, and the public at large have expectations about the kind of character types, narratives, denouements, plot twists, lines, tones of voice, and assorted dramatic devices that will appear in the performance. In asserting that, to paraphrase Shakespeare, "all the streets are a stage," we argue that the demands of the publicly viewed acting role and its contradictions to the police officers' private beliefs produce the essential tension that affects the principles, principals, and processes of modern law enforcement. That this was a visual ethnography assisted here, for the pictures were intended to show some of the displays and performances of cops and to provide data for introspective comment on the norms and forms of mediated representations of police officers.

THE DRAMATURGICAL METAPHOR

Anthropologist Victor Turner developed an interpretive schema, the universal "social drama," to explain the way that the tribal societies he observed handled periodic conflict at all levels of social organization, with different styles from culture to culture (Turner, 1982, p. 70; see also Turner, 1986). In general, social drama can and does occur repeatedly throughout all social levels, among drivers on the highway, customers waiting in line, research teams, families, villages, cities, nations, and beyond. Turner's point is that drama is a fixed feature of social life. It operates at not only the level of social drama but also at the level of genres of cultural performance, and the relationship between the two is referential. He goes on to say, "Paradigms of this type, cultural root paradigms, so to speak, reach down to irreducible life stances of individuals, passing beneath conscious prehension to a fiduciary hold on what they sense to be axiomatic values, matters literally of life and death" (p. 73). What he suggests is a two-way flow, life drama generating stage drama and vice versa.

Crisis or a breach of norms, ritualistic or anomical, is typically the situation that calls for the drama to unfold in response. The range of choices for dramatic expression and performance of social roles is both wide and limited. Suitable behaviors may be the offering of personal advice, informal arbitration, juridical and legal action, or the performance of a public ritual. In the instance of social dramas possessing a political twist, the main protagonist(s) are those whom Turner (1982) refers to as "star-groupers," individuals who

> manipulate the machinery of redress . . . the procedures of divination and ritual, and impose sanctions on those adjudged to have precipitated crisis. . . . [They] are the ones who develop to an art the rhetoric of persuasion and influence, who know how and when to apply pressure and force, and are most sensitive to the factors of legitimacy. (p. 72)

In this study, cops are star-groupers or, in shorthand, "stars" in the breaches of the peace of society: They must enact rituals of behavior to restore order, although they rarely can make things "right," that is, returned to the state antecedent to the crisis.

Mass media affect modern social drama. Television, for example, bowdlerizes all reality; compresses and contorts it; deletes some vast portions of human thought and action, entire societies, and whole professions; but abnormally focuses the small screen or the wide screen on some actions and some groups. Cops fall into the latter category. The "conscious prehension" of copness, of what it is to be a cop, the underlying presumptions of being a cop, and the range of possible actions open to cops are thus partly determined by the actors themselves or, more important, by the system that sustains and directs them. The quasi-mediated reality that permeates the culture is neither the result of top-down influence of mass media, nor is it a grassroots or organic assertion by physical beings outside of mediated space. To be a cop, to wear the dark uniform, the badge, and the gun, is to compete with a counterpart on the screen.

That screen presence enables the cop to think of his own life stance not only in terms of direct interaction through personal experience but also his projections of how other actors come to view him. Cops may be said to have a social role that is partly mediated, both through their own will and the will of others. Such a definition may be a subject of struggle, but it may also be a useful tool of survival, one of personal value enhancement. As we will see in the research conducted here and elsewhere, cops are both negative and positive about certain aspects of the mediated vision of police work. Although they, like any audience, might appreciate and thrill to the swashbuckling daring of the televisual hero cop, their own challenge to this stereotype is the potential disappointment of other actors in the environmental stage. What results is a

Figure 2.1.

subtle, reciprocal, reinforcing determinism between media and human being, especially, as in the case here, when the man or woman on center stage is also a frequent subject of mass media representations. They are stars in that at any scene they have the societal sanction to (literally) make thing happen. As one cop put it, "When I show up, I must take charge—that's what I'm paid to do, that's what people want." *PP:* "I must go through the door first. That's what I'm paid for" (see Figure 2.1). As activist stars, they impose their will (or try to) on the other players, driving narrative developments and conducting the rituals and routines; they see it as their job to take charge and tell people what to do (cf. Ericson, 1991) (see Figure 2.2). *PP:* "Part of the job is to get people to do things they don't want to do—even people who are big shots in their own life. But they must cooperate with me on the street." Cops perceive—and, more important, they perceive that others perceive—that the narrative must be carried by them.

Another important notion offered by the dramaturgical metaphor in general and by Erving Goffman (1959) in particular is the "team." Performances express mainly the characteristics of the task rather than those of the performer. The "performance team" or team refers to the concept of individuals who coordinate and cooperate in staging a single routine. Teammates display related reciprocal bonds of dependence and familiarity. The purpose of the team, a troupe of actors of sorts, is to establish a given definition of a situation. The teammate is depended on for his or her dramaturgical cooperation in this

Figure 2.2.

effort. It is a formal relationship, automatically emergent when one takes a place on the team but operates via informal agreement as a means of self-protection for the individuals. The nature of the reality performed is frequently reduced to a "thin party line" for the desired impression to be established. Public disagreement between team members incapacitates united action and "embarrasses the reality" supported by the team (Goffman, 1959, p. 86). Teammates are required to postpone the taking of positions that oppose the team line until they are out of public view; unanimity is called for to avoid the creation of "false notes" (p. 87). Establishing and maintaining a definition of the situation is central.

Each teammate must have access to information relevant to defining the team line or stand. Without this, a teammate may not be capable of asserting a suitable self to the audience. He must be "filled in." Not filling a teammate in can be interpreted as distancing him from the team or even setting him up for a fall. When a teammate makes a mistake in presenting the team stand, he is supported in public and taken to task when the audience is no longer present. Goffman (1959) finds this to be especially true in very authoritarian organizations. Superordinates maintain a show of unity at all costs, presenting a united front.

In most professions, standards of normative etiquette build up to the level of ritual, which aims to informally preserve a common or team front of the profession, distancing the profession from audience or clients, controlling information available to audience or clients, and maintaining professional boundaries. Control of the setting is important in determining the devices and strategies that can be used to limit the information available to the audience as well as giving a team a sense of security. In team performances, someone is usually given the position of director, the role of controlling the progress of dramatic expression and stimulating or sparking the show of "proper affective involvement" (Goffman, 1959, p. 99). Again, those with visualized leadership may not be those invested with dramatic and directive dominance. Some team-mates perform "purely ceremonial roles," having little else to do with moving the dramaturgical endeavor, and "are primarily concerned with the public appearance of the team" (Goffman, 1959, p. 99).

Cops are obviously a team. Street cops, as discussed later, often divide the world into the "we" (uniformed patrol officers) and the "not we" (everybody else). But not all teammates are equal, and it is only from a distance—the enaction of nonexperientially based stereotypes—that teams are indeed uni-form. Casts, cliques, and power hierarchies exist within even tight-knit groups; solidarity when confronting outsiders does not necessarily indicate seamless unity inside the team. Street officers may wear the same uniform and techni-cally be at the same rank, but they may develop their own patterns of differenti-ation and dominance. For example, one televisual and cinematic formula that I found essentially replicated among the St. Louis Park (SLP) officers was ath-leticism (see Hageman, Kennedy, & Price, 1981). With obvious exceptions, television's hero cops tend to be masculine, tough, quasi-athletic figures. It is only when they are purposely cast against type—Lacey, the Commish, and so on—that this characterization is abandoned. Within the SLP Police Depart-ment (SLP-PD), I found a cohort or perhaps a cadre of, for want of a better term, "pumped" cops. These were the cops who took seriously the physical preparation for the job. Almost all exercised regularly, lifted weights, or played some sort of informal contact sport. I perceived no differences in the characters of these cops from those on the rest of the force: Being fit did not mean that they were any more brutal or any less cerebral. Their conversational groupings, however, their extra-work friendships, tended to be with each other. This was assisted by the fact that they were generally not rookies but career cops in their late 20s and early 30s.

Athleticism was one basis whereby cops in this group tended to judge fellow officers. Negative characterizations were made against cops who were either too "geeky" or too "fat and lazy." One officer had a reputation for getting hurt too often and too easily. Such value judgments are not purposeless sniping. The fat and lazy cop, the unfit cop, the geeky cop, or the one who is always nursing some injury is deemed less likely to be of help in violent situations. But impression management also plays a role. Said one cop of another, "Perps [per-petrators, or criminals] must look at him and laugh. Anybody could outrun him." Such intragroup criticism borders on dysfunctional. It can, and in some cases did, seem to undermine group cohesion. On the other hand, police work is a physical activity, and I think that the fit cops would argue that not only is it up to everyone to keep up appearances and not "let themselves go," but also some spirit of competitiveness about physical fitness is actually beneficial for the department.

Finally, and most important as a part of the dramaturgical metaphor for this study, is Goffman's (1959, p. 112) definition of a *region*, that is, any place bounded by barriers to perception, to varying degrees. The front region (or "front stage") is any place where some aspects of the activity that occurs are accentuated and others are suppressed. Those suppressed might discredit or make impossible the success of the performance, the impression generated. A back region or "back stage" is the place where suppressed facts are likely to appear. Relative to a given performance, it is the place where the impression generated is "knowingly contradicted as a matter of course." This area serves many functions: the place where illusions and impressions for the audience are created, a place for a "team" (the inclusive group) reality check and schooling or reschooling of teammates who are not turning in a good team performance, and a place to step out of character, a zone of relaxation.

Regulation of the back stage is important in the process of *control.* In the back region, people attempt to separate themselves from the demands that surround them, to insulate themselves from outside determination. Back regions can be located in close proximity or even adjacent to front regions. Barriers between the two regions often provide little security for performers. Many humorous and not so humorous stories may be told about performers' comments and behaviors when they thought they were back stage but were still, at least partly, front stage. Embarrassment is the mild result, dismissal from job and estrangement from social group two of the more serious. Dialogue, as well as image, is important in maintaining the level of privacy "back stage." As described in Chapter 5, in street cop work, the back stage is the region where socially unapproved comments are made but also where, to a great extent, cops process and validate their own actions. One item for processing is the role of mass media in their lives.

APPROACHING COPS AS VIEWERS

Participant-observers adopt personas as much as do natives enacting their routines of public display. Mine, when in view of the public or in a group of officers, was to be as nondescript as possible, to stay in the background, if not the back stage. The cop was the star of the drama; I tried to observe as a bit player. Most of the time this seemed to work; sometimes it broke down, and a stage light focused on me. One late night, in a group of seven cops taking a coffee break, the one with whom I was riding told all the others, "Dave's doing a book about me, or at least he will if I kill somebody on camera for him." Other cops offered to help, giving advice on how the shooting should take place. I grinned, but I was made uncomfortable by being the subject of dissection, albeit casual, by the natives. In another incident, the department's SWAT (Special Weapons and Tactical) team, made up of ordinary officers specially trained, readied to storm an apartment where a reportedly deranged man had been making threats against cops and his neighbors. The team began evacuating nearby apartments and those in the line of fire. A cop knocked at a door; a woman with a baby answered. He explained quickly why they should leave the area. I took their picture as they ran away. The woman looked at me in terror, and I regretted the decision to photograph her. Have I added to her plight? Did she worry for a moment that she might be on the front page of some newspaper, barefoot, in an undersized T-shirt, holding a crying baby dripping pablum? In both cases, I got a sense of what it was like to be suddenly "on stage," and, notably, I was not rehearsed or ready for it as cops are.

Dramaturgical modes of analysis of human behavior put a stress on action as revealing less inner motivation than socially sanctioned display, what actors are encouraged to do, in certain situations that are ritualized, routinized, or preplanned. Such routines seem to permeate police work; so many scenes cops present, front stage or back stage, are surfeit with ritual. Without my notes and pictures to distinguish them, most car stops now merge in my mind; few are distinctive. What the cop did, what the driver did, what the cop said, what the driver said—there were only so many possible stimuli and responses. Yet, the paradox of police work is that this routinization can at any moment be shattered by the unexpected and the fatal. As one officer told me, "When a cop gets shot, it's often when he least expects it." Indeed, most cops see little actual violence but always live in a world that may potentially become violent. No matter how simple, sane, and safe the rituals of public display are, the world may destroy them and bring the curtain crashing down.

It follows that to understand police work in its own terms and in relation to mass-mediated imagery and its quixotic influences, we have to look at police behavior as embedded rituals, ones that reach beyond performance to living justifications, not only of ego but also of group solidarity. In examining the front stage, an ethnographer should try to gauge the reaction of others to the cops' performance and measure how cops adjust that performance and try to define their role in the most efficacious manner possible. In turn, the participant-observer ethnographer attempts to penetrate the back stage, to witness, listen to, and in this case photograph what is said and done when the chief, the citizens, and the bad guys are not watching or in earshot. It would be wrong, however, to overvalue the back stage as the site of revealed truth and counterpoise the front stage as the site of false posing and routinized dissembly. Lies and truths and all the shades in between, postures and visceral actions, and consciousness and self-consciousness are enacted both in public and in private. The fundamental question of this ethnography and any that seeks to identify the interplay of media and extramedia realities is how all the players in all occasions view their life situation in relation to the content, form, and effects of televisual and cinematic portrayals of their own kind.

Cops are not isolates: Like actors, they play to audiences and follow scripts. Where those scripts are written, the audience's preconceived expectations when they witness the cops' performance and react or try to modify it, and how the cops offer and alter their style and substance, orientation and action, and words and deeds are not the result of rigid deterministic forces. Neither do they originate from within the individual, untouched by materialist and cultural influences. Although the public, their colleagues, and the tangible world that cops inhabit affect their performance, it is also likely that mass media factor in as well. The real cop does not exist independently of the mediated cop.

Moreover, the televisual experience is the most common way in which people learn things, accurate or fanciful, about cop work—and it provides the key words for negotiation and dialogue. Whenever I speak to audiences, students, or colleagues about my ethnography, I always ask a simple question: "How many of you have had a long conversation, 43 minutes or more (the length, excluding commercials, of a 1-hour dramatic TV series) with a street cop about his life and work?" The only affirmative answers I ever get are from criminologists or from students whose father, uncle, or other relative was or is a police officer. Crucially, in almost no case has anyone ever viewed cops at length, in real time, face to face, in the back stage. So we have almost no contact with real live police officers, and, if it occurs, it is usually brief and in some moment of inconvenience and irritation (being stopped for a moving violation) or after a trauma (being mugged). In contrast, police permeate the world of media, and we the audience have great para-familiarity with legal procedure, the inside of the squad car and the precinct, and the codes and secrets of police and detective work. To answer the cliché "where's a cop when you need one": There's always one on TV.

Needless to say, concern with *how* law enforcement is portrayed in media is longstanding and, as described in the next chapter, originates in the pretelevision era. In the old Hays Code of cinema (the self-regulatory Motion Picture Production Code), one of the governing rules was that "the law shall not be defeated."[1] Criminals might be temporarily successful in their actions, but in the end they would pay for their crimes, and the long arm of the law would triumph. This rule, ironically, offered producers a cynical opportunity to rationalize sensationalism. Criminals could be shown gleefully robbing and killing innocents and enjoying the high life of gambling, boozing, and (implied) illicit lovemaking, yet as long as they died in a hail of bullets or took the long walk to the electric chair by the closing credits, the social order was deemed rescued and restored.

In addition, the American cop film (and TV show) was especially characterized by the notion of a single "man who stood alone" or a dyad of cooperating policemen—agents of authority, yet outsiders. The deviant hero is the tough guy, the loner, the man who will not go with the flow, who flouts conventional wisdom, who angers his superiors.[2] This profile, although less common in ensemble dramas such as *Hill Street Blues,* nevertheless is an important mythic element in the mediated and cultural substance of the cop's image. An example from the emblematic Clint Eastwood vehicle *Dirty Harry* was specifically the topic of a lunchroom conversation of police officers during my ethnography. The cops' views on violence will be dealt with in future chapters, but here they agreed that Harry Callahan was a model of the hero cop: unconventional, bold, action oriented, brilliant but anti-intellectual, infuriating to superiors, and a terror to criminals (see Ray, 1985). In a famous scene, Harry is seated at a lunch counter eating a hot dog. Looking out the café window, Harry asks the cook to call a certain number and report that a bank across the street is being robbed. How can he tell? As the hero, he *sees* the truth: a car parked outside the bank, the color of its exhaust, the pile of cigarettes, the "look" of the driver (he and his accomplices are all black, but Dirty Harry is an equal opportunity telepath). He mutters to himself, chomping on the hot dog, "Now if they can just wait until the cavalry arrives." Of course Eastwood, the lone man, *is* the cavalry. Bank alarm bells ring. Harry, half a hot dog stuffed in his cheek, temples pulsing with irritation, strides into the street.

And the gunplay begins. The shotgun-wielding robbers emerge from the bank. Impassively, Harry confronts them. Passersby scream, panic, and run in all directions, but the hero is a rock, unflinching even when grazed by a bullet or brushed by a speeding getaway car. He guns down the robber gang one by one. Then there is that great moment of cinematic charisma. A wounded criminal lies on the ground. Harry walks up to him, his .44 Magnum—"the most powerful handgun ever made"—extended. Several cuts between the men's faces heighten the suspense. Harry says coolly, "I know what you're thinking. Did he fire five shots or six? To tell the truth, in all the commotion I've lost track myself. The question is, punk, do you feel lucky?" The prone man considers and begins to reach for his shotgun, then draws away. As other police pull up, the thief calls out, "Hey, man, I gots to know!" Eastwood turns, points his gun at the man's face, and fires. The empty chamber clicks as the robber cringes in sweaty terror.

In the squad room discussion, what was revealing was not that real cops dismissed the density of the events. Would a cop really continue his lunch though he knew a robbery was in progress? It would have been wiser, considering the crowds of people in the area, to let the crooks get away and tail them, especially since Harry was in civilian attire. Would any real cop fire a gun, even one he knew was empty, at an unarmed wounded man's face? "How would that look on the 5 o'clock news?" asked one officer. The incredulities can be catalogued, but they are not the point. The cops appreciated the aesthetics of the presentation and Eastwood's characterization of "the baddest cop in town," but the commentary revolved around how, as one police officer put it, "That's what they [the public] see when they go to a movie. Then they look at us, and we're not that." Another stated, "Dirty Harry is everywhere, but they [mediated cops] have gotten a little wimpier." Another disagreed, "There are still tough cops out there on TV. *Hunter,* for example." Another concluded to general agreement, "Dirty Harry is what people remember."

At this point, although it was not my method to interrupt group conversations with questions, I did ask what they felt people thought about the Dirty
Harry cop, to relate media content to their view of their own environment. The
answer one of the police officers gave me seemed to speak for the room: "I
think they look at somebody like Eastwood and say, 'Well, he gets the job done.
He does it.' And they don't say, 'I want one of these guys driving my school
bus.' But they do want a tough cop to make everything better for them" (cf.
Klockars, 1980). Another officer added, "In 2 hours; faster on TV." Another
concluded, "And they think we can go around shooting anything that moves,
we're all on the edge, edgy guys with guns." As will be developed later, the
cop-as-savior, as enforcer of justice and as antiprocedural lone man, is exactly
the kind of image that the police believe is held by the ordinary public. Whether
or not that third-person assumption is correct, it influences police attitudes and
behaviors.

THE FOG OF THE STREET

Whatever the influence of media over our beliefs and behavior, we cross each
day a liminal threshold between social reality and parasocial reality. The border
between popular culture and ordinary life is indistinct: Influences crisscross,
merge, and meld. After spending 2 years riding around in a police car, I believe
that this is true for street patrolmen as well. It is less a question of how they or the
public are affected by TV than how they live in a television-infected world, a
world in which people grow up watching 6 to 7 hours a day of television, with
portrayals of law enforcement and criminality in news and entertainment. The
ethnographic method can delve into this issue in a way unlike either laboratory
studies or social surveys, allowing the researcher to let the subjects reflect and
react to the changing circumstances that shed light on the problems at hand as
those events occur and in retrospect.

Such issues and tensions affect both police officers and the individuals with
whom they come into contact. Cops live in a real world of law enforcement and
criminality; their knowledge about cop work is personal, physically experienced. Yet, as will be emphasized, police work is often conducted in a setting
analogous to what Clausewitz called the "fog of war." Cops must make rapid
life-and-death decisions based on scant data and Delphic reports—especially
about the people they encounter or are about to encounter. For example, officers often arrive on the scene of a call unsure of what to expect. A house alarm
has been set off: Is it the wind, a cat, or an armed intruder? In a crowded sports
bar on a Friday night, a "man with a gun" has been spotted by an anonymous
caller: Is the man a genuine threat, or was the call a prank? Or, late at night, a
car is stopped, and the long walk to the driver's door begins: Will it be a confused grandmother or a sociopath with an uzi?

At the same time, the cop world is a riot of variables and input data. There
are many people talking at once; also added is the burden of layers of official

Figure 2.3.

procedure. Included as well are traditions of tales and advice (Trujillo &
Dionisopoulos, 1987), memories of past experience, and the prejudices of
society and culture. In addition, and in line with the dramaturgical perspective,
the cop is often at center stage; other people look to him or her to *do something.*
That something is to solve their problems even if the solution is extrajudicial
(Black & Reiss, 1970; Sykes, 1975).

Finally, cop work, like almost no other vocation (except, with less consequence, sports), is the subject of much ex post facto scrutiny; cops know that
what they do will be judged by others, perhaps even resulting in the loss of their
livelihoods. It is small wonder, then, that one consistent theme I found in police
descriptions of their own world is that they feel like an "outsider" group, both
in the materialist sense ("criminals and lawyers are in charge, we just work
here") and the phenomenological projection ("nobody really knows us").

An incident I witnessed and photographed dealt with such issues. It was my
attempt to visually convey the "fog of war" of police work, the kind of dis-
parate content cops must analyze in their own street environment every shift.
On the street, unlike in the laboratory, no stimulus stands alone. In the photograph presented in Figure 2.3, an officer talks to a teenager sitting underneath a
railroad bridge. The wall behind them is covered with graffiti, much of it gang
signs and rebellious expletives. The officer, hands in pockets, spoke to the
young man for 20 minutes. He said the two "just talked. Looked like he needed
somebody to talk to." He reflected also, "We don't get to speak to them often
before they do something, before they get into trouble." By "we" he meant

cops, separate from the intercession of others, including parents. *PP:* "Look at all those gang signs—my competition."

But even though they are not social workers, cops still speculate about social forces, and they can, time permitting, intervene. The older man stands talking to the younger man; it is referenced as a father and son scene. Police often comment on how they feel when they are asked, indirectly by teenagers themselves and directly by some parents such as divorced mothers raising teenage boys with fathers absent, to be a father figure. An officer muses, *PP:* "Both parents are out of the house working all day. They come home late. They have no idea what their kids are doing. They don't want to know, and they don't want to talk about it." The cop sometimes is the only one for the kids to talk to. "It's me there at night by the side of the road," commented another, "not the reporters, not the judge—no criminal lawyers ever come out to crime as it happens." The cop, then, feels that being there makes his view authoritative and authentic.

This is another perceived intrusion of mass media into the cops' job and life. The TV cop knows where to find himself in the landscape of crime and law enforcement; closure comes before the final commercial, and if the bad guys are not actually convicted, they are at least identified. As will be expanded on later, this heroic (and psychic) televisual and cinematic cop adds to the burdens of the real-life officer while providing an appealing and amusing counterpart. That cop does not operate in the fog of the street, and his challenges, especially those of paperwork and ex post facto analysis by lawyers and others, are minimal. The real cop, then, finds the stimuli and intrusions that obscure his ability to accomplish his job heightened because of the standards that are created by the mediated outsider. Because we are all pseudo-experts on cop work, we fail to appreciate this central point: Cops really do feel that their *lived* experience counts much more than our mediated ones. Because we do not know the difference, they end up feeling much less respected as "stars" than they deserve to be. For this they do not blame television with any degree of bitterness, but they do see it as a prime suspect in the degradation of the value of their work.

NOTES

1. O'Hara (1961) ties many of the stock stereotypes that comprise formulaic media content to the dictates of the Television Code of the National Association of Radio and Television Broadcasters and to the Production Code of the Motion Picture Producers and Distributors Association of America—the Hays Code. Such codes are best viewed as the result of negotiations between public interest groups critical of media fare, state legislatures, and a Congress whose constituencies include outraged and active interest groups, and industry officials, themselves anxious to avoid state censorship and regulation (cf. Barnouw, 1990; Jowett, 1976; Sklar, 1975).

2. The characteristic persona, attitudes, and preferred modes of action of the TV western hero are almost identical (Parks, 1982; Wright, 1978).

Prime-Time Crime and Street Perceptions

The U.S. Department of Justice estimated that in 1996, about one in five Americans age 12 or older "had a face-to-face contact with a police officer" (U.S. Department of Justice, 1997). This number, however, reflects *any* contact, even the most brief request for directions; only one third of the contactees were classified as "victims or witnesses to crime."

In contrast,

> The typical American child is exposed to an average of 27 hours of TV each week—as much as eleven hours [a day] for some children. . . . That typical child will watch 8,000 murders and more than 100,000 acts of violence before finishing elementary school. By the age of 18, that same teenager will have witnessed 200,000 acts of violence on TV including 40,000 murders. (Subcommittee on the Constitution, 1990, p. 8)

The average American watches up to 7 hours a day of television; an American child will watch TV for about 1,500 hours a year; he or she will sit in a classroom for only 900 hours a year (Subcommittee on the Constitution, 1990; see also Greenberg, 1980, p. ix; Nielsen Report, 1995).

It follows that if people have grown up with TV, they have also grown up watching TV cops, from the earliest days of *The Plainclothesman* and *Dragnet* through *Adam 12* and *The Mod Squad* to *NYPD Blue* and *Real Stories of the Highway Patrol.* Programs depicting some part of or persons in the legal system, crime, or law enforcement have never dominated prime time (see appendix), but neither have they suffered from the waning in popularity of other genres, such as the western (Brooks & Marsh, 1995, pp. x-xxi).[1] Especially throughout the 1970s, 1980s, and 1990s, they have been a large presence in prime-time fare.

Admittedly, in terms of character, occupation, method, and demeanor, not all TV cops are created equal. Richard Diamond was not Joe Friday, Joe Friday was not Bumper Morgan, Bumper Morgan was not Doberman, Doberman was not Hunter, Hunter was not Barney Miller, Barney Miller was not Renko, Renko was not Lacey, Lacey was not Ironsides, Ironsides was not Tubbs, Tubbs was not Elliot Ness, Elliot Ness was not Danny Sarturo, Danny Sarturo was not Rockford, Rockford was not Starsky, Starsky was not Chin Ho, and Chin Ho was not Sipowicz. In addition, a majority of TV "cops" (at least the main characters of the series) were and are technically not street or uniformed officers but rather plainclothes detectives or private investigators (see Table A.3 in the appendix) (cf. Brooks & Marsh, 1995, pp. 1166-1215). In fact, shows whose main characters are nonranking, uniformed patrol officers or deputy sheriffs (e.g., *Adam 12* and *CHiPs*) number only a handful in the history of television.

Nevertheless, previous research has uncovered reasonably stable patterns in the activities, character types, and ideological import of the cop show as a genre. The purpose of this chapter is (a) to review, synthesize, and comment on what is known about the content of mediated cop representations and (b) to lay out what the research and the cops interviewed for this ethnography represent are the main convergences and divergences between mediated reality and street reality and, furthermore, to describe how cops think these affect the beliefs of the public and commensurably their own behavior.

TELEVISUAL CONTENT

One of the first studies to consider the content of portrayals of TV law enforcers was conducted by Dennis O'Hara in 1961. Interpreting themes, formulas, and stereotypes developed on television entertainment programming, he noted that the media view of law enforcement was somewhat contradictory. Police and police officials were generally depicted as honest, efficient, and intelligent, and the methods they used to apprehend criminals and bring them to justice showed the police as "almost infallible." In counterpoint—what is probably less true today—lawyers were depicted more often as villains than as heroes and as manipulators of the law whose motivation was primarily selfish. The tendency to associate goodness with supporting the status quo and badness or evil with circumventing or challenging the established social order was prevalent across media and media formulas portraying crime. In 1950s television, O'Hara concluded, to be good was to be law abiding; to be bad was to be law breaking and selfish.

The 1960s saw the inception of one of the longest-running and most fruitful studies of television content, that of George Gerbner and his colleagues at the Annenberg School of the University of Pennsylvania (Gerbner, 1969, 1972, 1980; Gerbner & Gross, 1980; Gerbner, Gross, Morgan, & Signorielli, 1980,

1982, 1994). This research was undertaken on the premise that commonly shared social values and norms are encoded into programming to serve the commercial television industry, attracting and maintaining the attention of the broadest possible audience. In turn, this homogenized television content is then further integrated into society, cultivating and reinforcing commonly shared values and beliefs among viewers, most especially among heavy viewers of television. Gerbner and his colleagues' yearly analyses have found portrayals of violence to be a pervasive, persistent, and highly effective strategy for symbolizing cultural values and norms and power relationships within society.

More specifically, television's world of crime and law enforcement was saturated with violence, but due process was rarely a feature.[2] With slight variations, the level and profile of violence in crime and action television programming remained stable between 1967 and 1978. "Good guys" frequently resorted to violence to keep order; law enforcers were many of these. Although it was not a subject of content analysis, we can draw from such findings that TV cops are generally aprocedural or antiprocedural; they are not form filers, and indeed, as is almost cliché, they rebel against the minutiae of "office work" by "pencil pushers." They are action oriented, with violence being their preferred action and problem-solving technique. Television cops, Gerbner notes, live in a "scary world" or "mean world" that heavy viewers assume reflects the true state of the real world.[3]

In the mid-1970s, Joseph Dominick surveyed portrayals of police and crime in prime-time crime drama and comedy and noted television's heavy emphasis on law-and-order programs, as well as television industry and police anxiety over the educational and socialization potential of television (Dominick, 1973). Where possible, he related patterns of portrayal to official crime statistics to assess their accuracy (although statistics, as cops themselves attest, are not automatically accurate standards of street reality). Dominick found the following patterns in 51 regularly scheduled crime programs on network television for the week of February 22 to 29, 1972.

1. TV crime is unsuccessful; 90% of crimes on television are solved by program's end. In contrast, only 23% of FBI indexed crimes were reported as solved.
2. Violent crime, especially murder, is overrepresented on television, vis-à-vis murder in real life.
3. Whites are overrepresented as perpetrators of crime. Blacks, young people, and lower-class individuals are underrepresented.
4. Whites are overrepresented as victims of violent crime.
5. Seventy-five percent of victims of attempted murders on television were police officers in major roles.
6. Little of the legal process is shown in television crime programs. On TV, the legal process usually ends with arrest.

7. TV police are seldom represented as villains (2% of the time).

8. Law enforcers in major roles usually commit violent acts (92% of the time). Sixty-four percent of law enforcers committing violence were also recipients of violent behavior.

9. On television, there is little violent crime among family members (7% of violent TV crimes). In real life, 25% to 30% of violent crime takes place within a family context.

The continuity between some of the structures of the Hays Code and Dominick's conclusions is self-evident: There is a moral order in the universe, where the wicked are eventually punished. Police on TV are active agents for bringing about the restoration of order. Their preferred method is, however, action oriented, with bureaucracy being eschewed. Basically, *cops are the most violent people on television.*

This is an important contextual finding in understanding the substance of the portrayal of law enforcement and criminality. The TV cop, after all, is a symbol as well as an assumed exemplar—and the latent message that violence solves all problems, including that of violence itself, may override nuances of good and evil. We may ask, Is the deviance of the criminal who commits violence, for profit, anger, or pleasure, truly deviant if the law enforcement officer's preferred tool to arrest this deviance is also violence? Does this connote that violence is not the problem as long as people who are approved, dramatically, as *good guys* are those committing that violence?[4]

The historical development of such paradigms is more difficult to gauge. There were two periods when crime drama was particularly prevalent in the prime-time television schedule (Estep & Macdonald, 1983). A surge of crime drama occurred between 1969 and 1971, and the genre's prominence reached a new height during the 1980-1981 television season. These terms notably coincide with the election of presidents Nixon and Reagan, who both ran on an anticrime, law-and-order platform; it may be that prime-time cops were following the agenda set by the oncoming administration.[5] But a top-down model of content formation need not be the only explanation. Both surges in crime dramas followed periods of civil disorder: 1968 was a watershed year of political assassinations, the Tet Offensive, student rebellions at home and abroad, urban riots, and rising crime rate. The late 1970s saw the Iran hostage crisis and the oil embargo. Television thus may have responded to public need for the assurance of law enforcement as much in popular culture as in the voting booths. It may be an incidental indication of the overlap between popular culture and political culture; each may affect the other. For example, President Reagan might call up a line from a Clint Eastwood "Dirty Harry" movie, *Magnum Force,* and invite opponents to "make my day." At the same time, a concomitant variable may affect the content of both politics and prime time: the public need for simple solutions in a confusing, frightening world.

Estep and Macdonald (1983) built on Dominick's (1973) work not only to assess the content of prime-time cop and crime programs but also to discern whether there was any substantive difference in the content of the above "high-crime" periods. They sampled prime-time crime from three television seasons—1976-1977, 1977-1978, and 1980-1981—and found that little had changed despite the addition of seven hourlong crime dramas to the network schedule. Their content analysis showed that television crime shows continued the pattern, prevalent since at least 1972 (as shown in Dominick's study), of overrepresenting violent crime.

Regardless of the crime, television perpetrators are most often caught by the police. In crime drama, murder suspects are arrested or killed, and 88% of robbery cases are closed by criminal apprehension. FBI records during these periods show that 72% of all murder suspects were arrested, but suspects were arrested in only 24% of robbery cases. Throughout the 1970s and into the 1980s, crime drama also consistently overrepresented police effectiveness. Television crime dramas continued to suggest that the motivation for violent crime was psychological and portrayed police as totally adequate in dealing with crime (Estep & Macdonald, 1983). Even those researchers noting that private detectives and sometimes private citizens were often more effective than police officers found law enforcers to be represented positively almost twice as frequently as negatively (Lichter & Lichter, 1983).

More recently, the broad-based and comprehensive *National Television Violence Study* (1997) uncovered similar patterns. The study is particularly notable for being designed to contextualize violent television content, that is, to describe and understand the posturing of violent content and to consider the effects of such posturing. Among its findings were that "bad" characters are punished for committing violence in 62% of all programming, but the punishment most often (40%) occurs at the end of the program—again reminiscent of the "ultimate decree" of the Hays Code. Only 23% of programs punish violence throughout the narrative, and 37% never or rarely punish the violent behavior of bad characters. The dramatic series is the genre featuring the highest incidence of punishment of violence committed by bad characters.

Another study more specifically addressed crime and criminality (Carlson, 1985). Carlson found that the world of prime-time crime (a) is highly unrealistic; (b) omits or distorts information about the criminal legal process; (c) presents morality plays in which legal compliance is an important norm and legal violations are always punished; (d) seldom considers constitutional rights of criminal suspects and treats civil liberties as technicalities hindering law enforcement while aiding dangerous criminals; (e) presents a multidimensional image of police as highly effective but sometimes incompetent, dishonest, or misguided and as too willing to use violence;[6] and finally, (f) portrays the world as a dangerous place where citizens must be constantly vigilant if they are to avoid becoming victims of serious crime.

In a separate study, Carlson (1983) surveyed 6th through 12th graders from eight public and private schools in the Providence, Rhode Island metropolitan area. Results showed crime program viewing to have a small but persistent influence on students' perceptions of the legal system, supporting the cultivation hypothesis. Carlson identified 39 instances along eight variables in which the mainstreaming effect was to be *expected.* He found evidence of mainstreaming in only 12 (30.8%). He advanced the spillover hypothesis to explain his findings. In this model developed in literature on political socialization, it is common, for example, for orientations toward political authority to spill over to orientations toward the larger political system. Furthermore, a sequence may develop between the variables in the spillover chain. Carlson found that crime show viewing, authority orientations (here, views of the police), and community orientations (fear of crime and perceptions of a mean world) acted independently to affirm the legitimacy of the status quo, the political system.

Carlson (1983) argues that crime shows do little to socialize citizens in the spirit of the democratic creed or to build an informed citizenry that is willing to question authority. But such findings do not necessarily mean that authorities will be supported: Indeed, the feedback loop suggested by cops themselves becomes evident. Carlson asserts that these findings have troublesome implications for the police and the operation of the criminal justice system. The public may develop unrealistic expectations of police effectiveness at the same time that it becomes anxious about crime and demands higher levels of police protection. If the police cannot meet public expectations, police-community relations, already a cause for police concern, may deteriorate further. This ethnography's findings confirm such fears.

A final pertinent work is Richard Sparks's (1992) *Television and the Drama of Crime,* in which he considers the role of portrayals of crime in public life in the United States and England. Sparks's study moves mass media criminology to new terrain, considering the role of crime drama in contemporary Western society. He examines the dramatic crime entertainment programs that are highly prevalent in our (British and American) nightly television schedule as satisfying moral tales and considers whether cop shows stimulate fear of crime, mystify the truth about policing, or fuel punitive attitudes toward criminals. For Sparks,

> to analyze "violence on television" is thus to take issue with the whole rhetoric. . . .
> Is it the case that at the level of our daily pleasures some forms of narration act
> against lucidity by superimposing on the real sources of our needs and anxieties a
> simplistic, diverting closure? (p. 119)

Sparks's (1992) work is wide-ranging, but of most relevance to this study is his argument that programs within the genre of crime drama have many similar and easily recognized elements:

1. Crime drama typically depicts social disturbances in urban settings.
2. There is typically a narrative sequence of danger and pursuit, framed at either or both ends by familiar and safer conditions.
3. The portrayal of heroism is central. The hero is usually male and possesses qualities of independence, individualism, ingenuity, courage, and strength. He must further display integrity and be decisive.
4. Heroes, not organizations, ensure justice. Thus, the hero policeman gives validity to the organization.
5. Villains and villainy function to allow heroes to restore justice.

Sparks's (1992, p. 149) crucial point is that the effects of media practice are "subtle and oblique" and are to be found in ordinary daily routines, conversations, and shared activities. Ethnography is well suited to connect to such activities, for in listening and observing both back and front stage, the content of the cop's environment can be not only described but also explained by those officers who live in it and mentally map it.

STREET PERCEPTIONS: POLICE RESPONSES TO THE SCREEN

Street cops live in a mean world. It is one partly of their own making because distrust is a survival trait. It is also an objective material reality that is premised on the relative scale of meanness a cop witnesses and contends with as opposed to that of the ordinary middle-class person. To understand how mean the world is, it is worthwhile to note how jarring my entry was into it.[7] I lived in St. Louis Park (SLP) a year before I began my ethnography of its police officers. My impression of the suburb was positive: easy access to freeways, good shopping, polite denizens—a pleasant but not extraordinary city. My apartment building was 4 blocks from the police station, bordering a neighborhood largely composed of Hasidic Jews. I never saw any crime; indeed, with the exception of traffic accidents, I never saw any social traumas or tragedies. My only awareness of cops was fleeting glimpses of their squad cars on the street and the infrequent distant wail of sirens. Although I was not a neighborhood activist or connected to community groups—I mostly commuted to other locations for work or entertainment—I still felt confident that I knew the city and was pleased with what I knew.

On the first patrol I ever took with an officer, he introduced me to the world that I did not know, yet it was the same one in which I lived. To him, it was a little joke: See what's going on while you sleep? To me, it was a revelation. He pointed out houses that contained wife beaters, corners on which rapes had occurred, and closed apartment shutters behind which lived pedophiles. The guy walking out of the Target store had been in and out of jail for petty thefts, but it's Minnesota, and petty thieves don't stay in jail long in Minnesota (this is what the cops told me).

Although battlefields are often marked, as Kipling said, "by the bones" of the dead or by stone markers, scenes of crimes are rarely memorialized. Sometimes, a family erects a small cross at the site of a traffic accident that has claimed their child's life, a women's group spray paints a red outline on the pavement denoting that "a woman was raped here," or a community group holds a "Take Back the Night" rally at the site of a vicious murder. But all these expressions are either private or ephemeral. Typically, the naive viewer— anyone who is not a cop—never knows what crimes were committed anywhere. As the months passed, I gained my own store of such connections to rapes, assaults, and burglaries, and SLP could never be the same for me. The world was not changed, but it acquired primed mental signposts that staked it out as full of menace.

The meanness of the street—reinforced by the cynicism and contempt that police at times feel for the public, their audience—is, like most prejudices, seemingly confirmed by the feedback of experience (see Figure 1.3). The aftermath to the incident pictured earlier was a case in point. When I next rode with the officer I accompanied on this call, he did not bring up the incident. When I asked, he said that he did not know what happened to the woman except that they had taken her to the hospital; he did, however, comment on "that jerk," her husband. The spiral of contempt is fed by the fact that cops encounter citizens at their worst, when they are either the victim of a crime or have recently committed one.

Yet, that cops see a mean world—as do heavy viewers of TV—does not imply that they think media reality is a mirror of truth. Police views of media representations of their profession and of law enforcement and crime in general vary according to the medium and type of programming. Several studies have found relations with, for example, news media representatives to be tepid or even antagonistic (Singletary & Stull, 1980). Whenever I have presented the findings of my research to law enforcement personnel, they have always expressed suspicion of the motives of editors and reporters (e.g., *PP:* "They're out to get us.") and academics (e.g., *PP:* "They don't understand us.").

Similar attitudes were expressed in ethnographic testimony. One of the frequent assurances I found myself having to make to police officers was that I was not a journalist. The nickname that several had for the local newspaper (the Minneapolis *Star Tribune*) was the "Red Star." They generally had a disdain for reporters for not understanding cops—that is, for being "Monday morning quarterbacks." Part of their reaction was due not simply to the content of media reporting about police officers but the fact that reporters are not "there"; reporters arrive after the fact and reconstruct a tertiary reality without authenticating the experience of the police officer. Also, there is the issue of negative coverage. Whereas reporters might see that there are "two sides to every issue," cops resent the idea that their word is doubted or considered no more valid than a suspect's. In a sense, cop values and news values collide, at least in the cops' estimation.

Attitudes about dramatic presentations of cops have also been studied. One survey found that police rated the media portrayal of police effectiveness to be most unrealistic (Arcuri, 1977). Their assessment, now two decades old, was that crime shows encourage compliance with the law and vastly overrate the effectiveness of the police. All crimes are solved in quick order. All crimes are continually worked on until they are solved. All departments have sophisticated equipment and methods with which to catch criminals. All fingerprints taken lead to arrest. Police always get their way—or can force their way. Never shown are crimes that go unsolved, murderers who are not caught, or crooks acquitted by a jury. One respondent commented, "The public thinks all goddamn crimes should be solved within a hour, even with commercials."

Police responding to the survey were especially critical of crime show portrayals of police as "supermen."

> The public gets the picture that cops are gods . . . and that every cop is on his own without any department supervision. Many crime incidents are blown out of proportion. . . . The average patrolman on the street may become involved in one homicide investigation in his career but cover 5,000 accidents. . . . He will probably never fire his weapon in anger in his entire career. (Arcuri, 1977, p. 243)

Respondents were also critical of the way crime shows portray the resources available to police for their investigations: "The uninformed public gets false impressions on the way police departments operate. They, the public, feel that all experts are at our fingertips . . . as well as all up-to-date crime labs. In most cases that's crap" (Arcuri, 1977, p. 243).

Drawing from previous research and confirmed by the observations and testimony of this ethnography and its subjects, the myths of mediated representations of police work can be briefly summarized and contrasted to street reality. Then the concordance or discordance between the two "effects" of cops and their work life can be sketched out into a set of perceptions of media content. All these notions will be elaborated on and clarified in the chapters to come, but they are useful to catalogue now as a baseline for understanding the link the cops see between TV and the street. The main themes include the following.

Level of Action

Media. Never a dull moment. TV cops are always, in the words of one of my informants, "doing something, or just about to do something, or planning to do something." If there is a pause on television, it is brief, or it is a pregnant pause, a moment of calm before the storm. Or it is a deliberative pause, propelling the narrative, creating a segue between scenes of drama and movement.

Street. Tedium and adrenaline. Street cops do not consistently experience action and high drama. There are dead nights when nothing happens or, rather, what happens would hardly pass the muster of a moment experienced by the television hero cop. Filling out forms is the norm. Action, when it occurs, is not part of a predictable plot arc but unexpected. It is generally agreed by researchers that uniformed police spend much more time counseling and in arbitrating disputes than actually dealing with crimes (Cumming, Cumming, & Edell, 1965; Ericson, 1982; Manning, 1988; Shadgett, 1990). By some estimates, as much as 97% of the patrol officer's time is spent on noncriminal matters or those that they or other members of the law enforcement structure have defined as not connected to a crime (Comrie & Kings, 1975; Ericson, 1982). Bureaucratic, administrative work takes up most of the patrol officer's activities (Ericson, 1982; Kinsey, 1985; Police Studies Institute, 1983; Shadgett, 1990; Webster, 1970). Even detectives, who presumably are more focused on matters that have already been classified as criminal activity, may spend half their time on office work (Ericson, 1993, p. 45).

Effects. Cops know that mundane file work and slogging patrols are the essence of good policing. On the other hand, they may very well define *authentic* cop work as fighting crime (see Ericson, 1982, 1993; Manning, 1977; Reiner, 1992, chap. 3). Media stereotypes encourage this latter view. However, the discordance between the stereotype and the reality creates some embarrassment for street cops when perceived by observers, including the ethnographer. In addition, being human, cops do not enjoy tedium, regardless of its bureaucratic necessity. They too seek out action and sometimes place value on "keeping busy." Indeed, they became cops not to file forms but, to some extent, to engage in the very activities that media cops overexemplify. A cop notes, "On TV, 90% of cop work is racing and shooting; in my job that's 1%." He adds, *PP:* "We must be pretty dull compared to them." Another cop responds to the question of the pace of TV: "It's breakneck—everything they do, they do it fast, before the commercial. What can I say, it's TV." And on TV, lag time is anathema, but on the street it is commonplace.

Escalation of Criminality

Media. Fighting (serious) crime is the mediated cop's business. As noted, crime, as well as its legal and extralegal aftermath, is the single most popular subject of factual and fictive television programming. More important for our purposes, mediated cops are shown as dealing with serious crime, which lends itself better to action and dramatic suspense. TV cops, for example, tend to investigate murders or other major crimes and very few mundane matters. There is, in essence, an escalation effect in which "serious" crimes involving loss of life or bodily injury are extremely common.

Street. The arrest, the trademark of the power of the cop, is itself much rarer than we would imagine. One study of New York City patrol officers, for example, found that up to 40% of them did not make a single felony arrest in a year

(Walsh, 1986). Rather than escalating matters into criminal activity, real-life police work often seems to be about preventing crime—that is, literally trying to reduce the number of incidents that become classified as crimes. For example, as few as 25% of calls to the police requesting service are actually forwarded to police officers; the rest are screened and routed elsewhere by dispatchers (Bercal, 1970; Jorgensen, 1981; Manning, 1988; Percy & Scott, 1985; Shearing, 1984). When an officer does respond, a substantial portion of the incidents are "classified down" to either noncriminal or minor status (Comrie & Kings, 1975; Ericson, 1982; Manning, 1988). As one cop interviewed for this study noted, "We don't want everything to be a crime; we have to deal with things on the street. We know they don't have much room in the jails."

Effects. Cops believe that people's assumptions about their job affect their job, especially in this dimension. Mediated cops do deal with the same kinds of events and issues that real cops do but in inverse proportions, so that mediated reality may be said to be inreal—that is, intensified reality—rather than unreal, showing preposterous events (Perlmutter, 1995). There is much of the latter as well, of course: A real crime scene investigator would laugh at the crime scene investigations on supposedly realistic cop shows, which portray everyone, from rookie uniformed officers to mayors, tromping around the crime scene, disturbing evidence. But essentially, because people think that cops are busy or should be busy "catching murderers and rapists," then the normal, undramatic aspects of police work, which are nevertheless essential to maintaining law and order and keeping the peace, are undervalued and almost unknown. A cop tells me, "When we stop a motorist and he tells me that I should be spending my time chasing murderers, it's ridiculous."

Level of Violence

Media. For the most part, mediated cops are violent men and women. They menace, fight, shoot, and kill, and they do so with relative impunity. Physical force, even brutality, is part of their tool kit for solving crimes and often the first resort in any situation in which their relentless quest for justice is stymied. The TV and cinema cops' world is ultraviolent and mean.

Street. Street cops also live in a mean world, but it is usually one of potential rather than result. They can be violent; people can be violent to them. There is always a chance they might have to shoot somebody; they never know who might pull a gun or a knife on them. But as any wildlife biologist would testify, the street cop would be extinct as a species if he engaged in the same amount of carnage as his mediated cousin.

Effects. I ask a cop, "If you could be any TV cop, which one would you be?" He shrugs and answers that they all live too dangerous lives. "I'd get killed in the [first episode] if I was a TV cop." Another cop tells me about going to speak at a grade school class. The kids are bright and bubbly, and they are excited to talk to a police officer. He tells them what to do if a stranger comes up to them, to make sure to look both ways before crossing the road, and so on. Then it is question-and-answer time. A prim girl of about 8 years asks, "How many people have you killed this week?" It is an innocent question. The cop later tells me he was tempted to say, "About 20. Next question?" But instead he explained that he had never killed anybody, never even fired his gun at anybody. "Fucking television" is the culprit behind the child's misconception. Street cops resent being perceived as naturally violent. They find humor in but are also contemptuous of the public's estimation of the body count they rack up in daily cop work. Yet, they understand that force and the threat of force are part of their job. Often seeing themselves as a thin blue line against barbarism, they understand that the barbarians cannot be held at bay by tea and sympathy.

Heroes and Villains

Media. Clearly defined good and evil. Mediated reality is often more textured than the categorization schemes content analysis allows. There are shades of gray in almost every portrayal of a police officer or a criminal, more so in acclaimed dramas such as *Hill Street Blues* and *Homicide: Life on the Street.* But in general, on television, as one cop put it, "you don't need a score card" to tell the good guys from the bad guys. Certainly, by the end of an episode, the audience knows who is in the right and who is in the wrong, having received unsubtle neon cues to cheer or jeer certain characters.

Street. The good, the bad, and the gray. Street reality offers a more complex tableau in that cops often meet good people who have done bad things and bad people who may be acting "good" because they understand how the system works. Stereotyping, however, is inescapable and in some ways matches the abbreviated characterizations of mediated forms. Police deal with people for only a few minutes, usually in the middle of an incident, and must instantly decide what to do, whom to arrest, and whom to release. The job calls for jumping to conclusions. Cops, however, unlike the television audience, rarely get any background or back-stage view of those they confront.

Effects. Much of police back-stage discourse and front-stage behavior attempts to valorize and validate their judgments about people. In the front stage, cops try to present a united front (Goffman's [1959] "team") but with a lead cop making decisions. In the back stage, conversation emphasizes the rightness of courses of action in most cases. Cops relate, however, that unlike on television, everyone in real life seems to conceive of themselves as aggrieved victims. They blame this on media—although this may seem somewhat contradictory. It is also part of a feeling that things are getting worse: "In the old days, most crooks admitted it when you got 'em." Now everything is relative, and everyone has a lawyer. It is not clear if cops perceive the graying of the world as the result of mass media effects or changes in society and culture itself.

The Status of the "Cop"

Media. Reverse-status hierarchy. On TV, the patrolman is often the dumb backgrounder, attendant, or ignorant foil for the detective hero. He is the guy who guards the door of the hospital room of the wounded victim. He is stupid or incompetent, whereas the plainclothes hero is a brilliant problem solver. He has little responsibility. The real, important work is done by lawyers and detectives.

Street. Street cops are "gatekeepers" of the criminal justice system (Alpert & Dunham, 1992). On the street, cops view their own status as patrolmen as the most important link in that system. They get there first and make the crucial early decisions. What they do, say, and touch affects the future of any case. They save lives, they keep the peace, and they do the dirty work that superiors and detectives do not handle. They are the "real" cops.

Effects. A paradox: Cops talk about their TV stereotypes; on the other hand, as said earlier, many of the characters who represent those stereotypes are not technically uniformed officers—they are detectives or private investigators or even lawyers. An officer notes, "The uniformed cop has the most responsibility in our work—but on TV he fetches and totes for the suits." Mass media's influences are generalized and specified at the same time, the public holding on in each case to that stereotype that reflects worst (the dumb street cop) and most exaggerated (the hero cop). Confounding the issue, cops believe that many elements act to take away their autonomy in making street decisions.

Omniscience

Media. The TV cop may make mistakes, may stumble up a blind alley, or a hunch may play him wrong, but overwhelmingly he uncovers the truth, to the point of almost psychic awareness of what other people are thinking, what they have done, where the clues are, and what is going on out of sight. His omniscient outlook allows him to act in defiance of procedure and yet triumph because of his mental powers.

Street. "We know, but. . . ." Street cops equally believe that they know a great deal about what other people are thinking and what they have done based on extremely little information. In part, this is a virtue brought about by a necessity. Cops are given almost no advance data about what they encounter on the street or on a call. They must also make up their minds quickly and resolve issues rapidly, but they are under great pressure to obey procedures set down by law and department policy. They cannot engage in the career-risking gambles of mass-mediated cops because they have not been assured the script will result in their triumph.

Effects. Cops perceive that the public, if not stereotyping them as dumb street cops, jumps to the other extreme and expects cops to be mind readers, to instantly know who is guilty and who is innocent. In doing so, the public fails to provide the kind of information that police really need to complete their business. The anticipation of omniscience undermines efficient police practice. "You show up at a scene, and people give you nothing to go on, and they expect you to know 'whodunit' in seconds [laughs], maybe before the commercial."

Closure

Media. There are almost no unsolved cases on TV. Even on *Unsolved Mysteries,* the producers provide strong implications—by selective presentation, narrative tone, and leading reenactments—of who is really guilty and what really happened. More typically, the cops "get their man," the bad guy goes to jail, and the case is closed.

Street. A middle but no beginning and no end. The street cop arrives when incidents are in progress. No camera can show him the back story, and often he will never see or even hear of the resolution of the case he confronts. More important, he perceives that the legal system rarely enacts closure, at least the kind of closure that an audience would be satisfied with. Bad guys are caught and tried but often manage to finagle a reduced sentence. Lawyers, like vultures, pick the case apart. The law may work itself out to a resolution, years later, but justice is rarely served. Above all, crimes are neither necessarily solved nor solvable. In this vein, one manual on criminal investigation contends,

> The fact that a crime remains unsolved does not indicate a deficiency in the investigation; nor does a conviction of the accused necessarily mean that the investigation was conducted in an intelligent manner. . . . [In fact,] it is a common misconception that every crime is intrinsically soluble; that there is always sufficient evidence available to reveal the identity of the criminal; that the perpetrator always leaves traces at the crime scene which, in the hands of a discerning investigator or technician, will inevitably lead to his door. [Hence the public may be] indignant at the inability of his police force to locate unerringly the perpetrator of a mysterious bank robbery among several million inhabitants of his city. (O'Hara & O'Hara, 1994, p. 6)

Effects. The perceived discordance between mass media and fact here creates tremendous tension for the cops when they deal with the public, especially victims of crime. People want to be told that punishment will be enacted and that it will legitimately fit the crime. Cops know that this is almost never possible. It makes their work more difficult that people hold an optimistic expectation, but they also blame the system for not better providing a just resolution. *PP:* "People don't know how much our hands are tied. They think we can just go kick down a door, get their stuff back, and make it all better—well, maybe Hunter can do that in 10 minutes but I can't."

Focus

Media. Mediated representations of police work can have interweaving plots. This is especially the case in continuing series. However, although the director may give the impression of following two co-occurring actions using a split screen or through intercutting, generally the camera only shows one thing at one time. The event that is front stage eclipses all others, even if it takes place in the back stage. What is important is what is being shown; it is important because it is being shown.

Street. The street cop must consider multiple contexts no matter how focused he is on what is happening before him. The typical situation in SLP, unreflected by the television screen, is that only a few officers patrol a wide area in a relatively large population. Research on routine preventive patrolling has yielded both low and high estimates of its value in deterring or suppressing crime (cf. Cordner & Trojanowicz, 1992; Kelling, Pate, Dieckman, & Brown, 1974). But for cops and, by inference, the public, that a police officer can "be around" to answer calls in a timely fashion is a basic function of the profession.

Effects. Street cops cannot spend too much time on any one incident, investigate every suspicious activity, or avail themselves for as long as complainants wish. They literally have other things to do or need to be free in case other things occur. If they really did spend all of their time, as irate traffic violators sometimes goad them, "chasing murderers and rapists," the entire system of police response would collapse.

Exceptionality

Media. Although many TV police programs are able to portray the routine of work, there is an air of exceptionality to every situation. Because the viewer and the cop are relatively omniscient, they see through the haze of characterization to understand what people really want and what they really think. The cop pays attention and treats each problem uniquely.

Street. "We've heard that before." Street cops and this ethnographer become rapidly dulled by the repetitive character and scripts of people's excuses and explanations for breaking the law. There is no new excuse under the sun, and their dubious nature is further maligned by the fact that most are lies.

Effects. People, especially those who have a self-perception of being virtuous noncriminals, are incensed or at least irritated that the cop will not treat them as exceptional or will not instantly believe whatever story they tell or accept whatever excuse they give. They are unaware that behind them is an invisible queue (recalled by the cop) of thousands of others who, in identical situations, have offered up identical rationales for misbehavior.

Gravity

Media. Cops on TV have been comedians, and even in dramatic series there are moments of humor. Since the detective novels of the 1920s, the smart-aleck detective has been a staple of fiction (Chandler, 1950/1988, pp. 1-18). But humor and pathos tend not to be mixed up. A scene is either serious or funny; the twain do not meet.

Street. Always kidding around. As a defense mechanism and as a necessary desensitization to be able to go home at the end of the shift without fatal doses of stress and heartache, cops employ humor on a scale and frequency that would be surprising and disconcerting to the public. The joking in the squad room and between officers out of earshot of citizens is continuous and often ribald.

Effects. It was never expressed to me directly or even implied that cops keep their (darkly) humorous side from the public because of the influence of mass media and its emphasis on sobriety. However, it is an important dichotomy of the front stage and the back stage, between the public image of the cop and his private release. It is also quite understandable to them that the cop as jolly or morbid joker would be an unacceptable front-stage projection and one they probably would not want to play themselves.

Deliverers of Justice, Keepers of the Peace

Media. TV cops rarely deal with law; in fact, law is more often seen as antipathetic to justice—the legal technicality, for example, pulled by the shyster lawyer. The hero cop rather dispenses justice, makes things right, and avenges (by hook or by crook) wrongs.

Street. Caught between the public and the system, real cops must in most cases obey the law or at least not encourage or get caught themselves disobeying the law (Bittner, 1967). In turn, the law, because of its complexity, its overemphasis on the rights of the accused, and its glacial pace, has either no connection to justice or interferes with it. So cops are left in the unenviable position of enforcing rules they do not necessarily think work and certainly do not seem to make people happy.

Effects. The thirst for justice, no matter how old it is in human culture and tradition, is often ascribed to the false expectations created by mass media. Real cops feel they must compete as solvers of problems and dispensers of justice with their cinematic and televisual counterparts, who of course have tremendous advantages in this quest. Of all the ways in which people may feel that real cops do not measure up to the standards of mass media cops, this one is the greatest discouragement and irritant to the police officer.

Activities of the Back Stage

Media. Sanitized back stage. Television and cinema cops get raunchy, complain, and make disparaging remarks about the public, their superiors, and each other. But this is greatly cleansed from what goes on in the back stage in real life. No matter how crude a character, the "hero" TV cop rarely alienates an audience by making truly socially unacceptable statements as a common practice.

Street. Sex, lies, and stupidity. In real life, cops often make fun of, complain about, or criticize many of the people they encounter—in the back stage. For the uninitiated, this can seem shocking and brutal. Victims of assault, people in car accidents, someone whose stereo has been stolen, and of course all perps suffer such remarks. Moral judgments as well come fast and furious. People are stupid, jerks, and liars. The back stage is full of such remarks; they are, as I argue later, intensely functional and allow cops to relieve the tension of work. They are also part of most industries, from hamburger flipping to college teaching.

Effects. In some ways, this could be one of the few uniquely positive stereotypes of police, positive in the sense of making cops look good but also helping them in their work. The problem is when the back stage is penetrated—when what one cop says to another is overheard or is revealed in court testimony, through undercover journalism, or by a citizen behind a door. Ripped from its context of coarse humor and therapeutic maligning, such back-stage commentary is disconcerting, the more so when contrasted to the scrubbed-up mass-mediated image.

Chronology of Events

Media. Compression of time. In all mass-mediated representations of law enforcement and criminality—even the so-called reality-based show, documentary, or news program—events are compressed and edited to render swifter progress of the narrative and much more rapid resolution of the issues. Transitional events such as filing forms are culled; the long, dull sequences of ordinary cop work are either compacted into a few seconds or omitted.

Street. The forever war. In real life, cops understand—because they live through it—how long it can take for the system to resolve itself. A person might be arrested, but the case may not come to trial for years; after a conviction may come the appeal and a new trial. When rapid action does occur, it cannot be resolved in the interests of the public without the accompanying periods of stasis.

Effects. Self-consciousness here erupted in the ethnography, when cops often commented to me on how dull their work must seem based on, they assumed, my expectations from mass media. In a personal and structural sense, they resent the enforced lengthening of time by the system: "The law makes everything take forever."

Being There

Media. Comprehensive vision of audience. In mass-mediated visions of cop work, the audience is given godlike powers of observation. They can see clues kept from the cops, overhear secret conversations, perceive revealing facial close-ups, and receive voice-overs that give them insider information. Even when, in the interests of suspense, something is withheld, by the rolling of credits everything is eventually revealed to the viewer. In a sense, the audience ends up knowing more than the cops.

Street. "Thereness" of cops. Uniformed police are first on the scene. They see what no one else sees, they have been in the line of fire, and they see misery and blood at close quarters, and that gives them a primal perspective of what crime and criminality and their own work are "really like." No camera, especially wielded by some Hollywood auteur or tourist reporter, can capture the reality they see, nor is it regularly there to witness it. A connection of "thereness" exists in a story told by Michael Herr (1973) in *Dispatches,* the account of his Vietnam experience as a reporter. He describes meeting the remaining men of a long-range reconnaissance platoon that had just returned after a mission in the jungle. Herr asked one of them what happened. The soldier's reaction was monosyllabic and minimal: The man who had been there, who witnessed and participated in the action, had not the energy, the words, or the patience to recapitulate what happened on the mission. Instead, as Herr recounted, "he just looked like he felt sorry for me, fucked if he'd waste time telling stories to anyone as dumb as I was" (p. 6). Words are not sufficient, for they do not adequately convey the visceral impressions of being in direct view of what is happening or has just happened. Because of the "first on the scene" quality of the street officer's view of crime and law enforcement, his or her assessment of that view as privileged is heightened.

Police see crime as no one else does except the perpetrators and the victims. Even the most brutal crime cannot be fully re-created for a jury through a videotape of the scene, hospital Polaroids of the victim, an autopsy report, or the tearful testimony of relatives. This view was expounded to me at length by an officer, and his remarks are worth citing (*PP:*) in full:

> Whatever happens later, nobody sees it the way you see it. It's not like you can't take a picture and not get something out of it, but you're there, and you're seeing terror in people's faces, you're seeing how they're hurt, you're seeing how they're wounded, physically, and that can come out in a picture, but never in the same way that it is when you feel it in front of you. The same is true for the perps. They get to trial a year later and some lawyer has told them how to clean up, how to speak right, how to act in front of people. They don't see the same guy, stinking of beer, cursing the whole world, laughing at you, full of anger, fury, whatever, at the victim. Nobody sees that except us.

So, in a sense, media reality is an appropriation, a stealing away of the rightful property of the on-the-scene cop.

But "there" does not just mean being there. The soldier to whom Herr was speaking did not authenticate his own experience simply because he happened to be in one place at one time but because it typified a kind of event that no one who had not been there repeatedly, as a matter of course or profession, could understand. An incident without an image illustrates this point. At about 9 p.m., a ride-along showed up at the police station. This transient observer was a defense lawyer who wanted to see some police work "up close"; he spent all of 2 hours in the car. The cop with whom he rode later told me, "Can you believe it? He thinks you can be a tourist for this kind of stuff." I cite this incident not to validate the ethnographic method, which claims knowledge only after thousands of hours of observation and experience, but to underscore that cops value their own perspective because they are "there" day in and day out. They not only have the patent on experience, but they have also earned over time the right and the means to contextualize that experience.

Effects. Cops are some of the few members of society who are sanctioned to use lethal violence in almost any *location*. I do not use the term *situation* because cops technically can shoot only with proper cause and then undergo, in most departments, a review of the shooting and its circumstances. But cops are authorized to kill or use force, whereas ordinary citizens may do so only in very limited circumstances (e.g., in defense against armed assault). Cops use violence as a part of their job and indeed would rebel if that right were taken away from them. They are also subject to much ridicule from those who second-guess police actions. An example is the query after a police shooting of a suspect: "Why didn't the cops shoot to wound?" As one cop put it to me, "I don't know how to shoot to wound." *PP:* "Only some grandmother who's never fired a gun or never fired a gun at a moving target that is firing at you could say something this dumb. Yeah, a lawyer would say it too, though they're lying because they should know better. The media, reporters, I don't know, but they must be too stupid to know."

That factor, that cops *know* whereas others do not because they cannot or will not learn or have not been there, contributes to group solidarity among the men and women in blue. It also places them in an almost unique societal position to comment on violence in media and its "realism." This dichotomy is the fundamental challenge to the self-perception of cops and their own estimate of their value to society. People think they know what it is like to be a cop because they have seen so many cops on TV and in films. Whether such portrayals are "realistic" is almost beside the point: Real cops live out complex work lives and have onerous duties that simply are not expressible in any other way than to be there among them, day after day, dog shift after dog shift. TV is not there, yet TV is with them, and they know it.

NOTES

1. The crime-and-cops genre has long been of interest to researchers. Several early studies analyzing television content found crime and law enforcement to be a major category. Examining television content on all seven New York City television stations, Smythe (1954) found drama to be the largest category of content and crime drama to be the most prevalent and rapidly growing type of drama, accounting for 10% of programming in 1951 and 16% in 1953. Twenty percent of television's dramatic characters were criminals; law enforcement officials were highly stereotyped, with police officers holding socially desired values, and lawyers were portrayed as the "dirtiest," "hardest," and "dullest" of professional character types. Another study, by Head (1954), examining 209 drama programs airing over a 13-week period, found 17% of characters were criminal and 17% of characters had jobs that pertained to police work.

2. The level of criminal violence declined, but violence committed by lawmen remained the same (Gerbner, 1969).

3. Some research has offered at least partial support to the scary-world hypothesis advanced by cultivation analysis (Barrile, 1980; Carlson, 1985).

4. It is a general feature of all "good" and "bad" males on TV, not just cops, to use aggression to solve problems (Nelson, 1985; Wynnejones, 1985).

5. The prominence of crime drama in these periods has been attributed to the political ideology of the Nixon and Reagan administrations, respectively (Estep & Macdonald, 1983).

6. Carlson (1985) finds that crime dramas that "emphasize the 'new realism' often portray the police as brutal or corrupt" (p. 153). One of the problems that Carlson generally has with the TV image of police is that it is so multidimensional. Which dimension does the public identify with, he asks rhetorically: police as Keystone Cops or Kojak?

7. Objectively, cop work is *not* more dangerous than agricultural labor, construction work, or mining and quarrying. But as Bayley and Bittner (1993) point out, higher rates of death in those fields are not the result of "willful" harm. Cops face attacks by strangers that are "personal, human-to-human, and imbued with malice" (Bayley & Bittner, 1993, p. 112). In addition, the researchers note that although few cops are actually shot, encounters with low-level violence (e.g., shoving, punching, kicking, tripping, biting) are extremely common.

Ethnography and Police Work

The mainstream impressions, ideas, and themes of mass media flow over and around us, to use Gerbner's (1969) powerful metaphor. The methodological goal of any study of a community of people embedded, as most are, in a mass-mediated world should then be to understand how the participants negotiate their status in that world. Cops make a good case population to study because their place in the media world, including its liminal thresholds, is prominent, ubiquitous, and inevitably of consequence to others and themselves. What cops think about their world and how the world treats them ultimately affects the lives of millions of others, both "perps" and victims. As one officer noted to me, not without some irony, "I can ruin anybody's day; I can also make something bad a little better."

But how do we understand the mediation of the social world for cops? This study tried one approach, participant observation. It is not original as a research method, although the main goal is unusual for a study of police work. Yet, in stepping back and looking at previous ethnographies of cops, we see many recapitulations and notations that equally point to media-related structuring and tensions in the daily thoughts and lives of police officers. The purpose of this chapter is to sketch out some of the relevant findings of previous research—which, in toto, suggests that the observations offered here are not unique to my study population, location, or time.

OBSERVING THE STREET COP

Sustained observation studies describing and analyzing general police work at the level of the street cop constitute by far the most prevalent and influential ethnographic approach to cop work, in contrast to the relative paucity of street cops as feature players in prime-time fare. Typically, such works make mention of the street cop's relationship to his or her superiors, but their focus is on the day-to-day experience of policing on the streets. In general, their findings across

space and time are quite similar. Rubenstein's (1973) *City Police,* set in Philadelphia in the early 1970s, is typical in this regard, although the author was a
reporter, not an ethnographer. Rubenstein mentions as a rationale for his study
that police are known mainly through stories of drama, action, and scandal in
novels, print and television news, comics, and television crime dramas. As part
of the research, he entered the Philadelphia Police Academy and was allowed to
join a patrol unit, working a 6-day schedule in several districts. Although he was
never sworn in as a police officer, he was able to take to the streets as an *armed*
observer, an extremely rare instance for any ethnographic context.

One of Rubenstein's (1973) observations concerns the discrepancy between
police training and on-the-job experience. He argues that a cop must be "on the
job" to learn the job. The notion pervading the text is that police work is lonely
despite the officer's contact with many members of the public each day. This is
shown to be a function of the police officer's role of potentially controlling all
those with whom he comes in contact. The police officer is aware of the ambi-
guities in his work, but he is unable to discuss them openly with those who have
not shared his experiences. Cops, Rubenstein maintains, do illegal things "in
order to fulfill obligations that are required of them . . . but it is difficult to
explain to outsiders, [for example] that a policeman may have to commit per-
jury in court because the people he arrests, their lawyers and prosecutors may
tell lies" (pp. 435, 436). The few close friendships he may form are likely to be
with other police officers, for they are the only ones who can fully appreciate
his situation. (From a dramaturgical perspective, we might also add that other
cops are the only people consistently allowed into their back stage.)

Rubenstein (1973) also examined the cops' status as an authority figure.
The policeman is given a great deal of power, and the public *wants* him to exercise it. Once a policeman is permanently assigned to a sector, his education
really gets under way. He spends his time on the job observing and learning all
he can about his beat, geographically and in regard to the people and businesses he is responsible for protecting. The experiences of police studied
indicate that they view successful policing as acquiring bits and pieces of
knowledge, information, and experience that they can put together to become
self-sufficient and effective, as well as valuable to their colleagues. They have
a great deal of discretion within the preserve of their sector. They spend much
of their day making judgments regarding interactions with people in the sector,
learning over and over how to assess requests made of them, information given
to them, and situations that they happen upon. The judgments cut across race
and class lines and are evaluated in terms of local legitimacy, what is legitimate
police work and police concern in their sector of the city. Decisions must be
made quickly and without the advice of the sergeant. Officers learn that they
cannot trust what they are told. They continue to be aware of this long after
developing techniques for assessing the validity of claims made on them.

P. K. Manning's (1977) ethnographic study of British police, although
reported in the language of anthropology and sociology, essentially makes

similar conclusions. Manning set out to determine "who defines this work, sets its level and standards, enforces its definition of mistakes and excess, and constructs its social reality" (p. 15). He also employs the dramaturgical metaphor as a tool for interactional analysis and conducts an organizational analysis. His reason for the latter is his commitment

> to the notion that social life is both fragile and negotiated—is built up and affirmed almost daily in interactional encounters—while at the same time appreciating the pattern in life that comes from the inertia that social structures possess and are continuously granted. (p. 15)

Manning notes that at the time of his observational fieldwork, police had recently felt the need to determinedly pursue the public confidence. But this is only one reason why the police need to "dramatize the appearance of control." It is a necessary construction if they are to save their reputation of "secular sacredness" and if they are to give a performance worthy of convincing their various audiences that they are fulfilling their obligation of controlling crime and maintaining public order.

Manning (1977) suggests some basic themes of policing symbolized in public, ritual portrayals of and by the police:

1. The presence of a civil body politic in everyday life symbolizes the capacity of the state to intervene and the concern of the state for the affairs of its citizenry (see also Shils, 1950).
2. The continuity of society via police is a visible attachment to traditional values of patriotism, honor, duty, and commitment.
3. The police, in their role of enforcers of rules, laws, and norms sanctioned by the state, come to connote secular sacredness and authority. This relationship with an absolutist state morality connects the police image to that of the state and its symbols, elevates the rule of the state in civil life to centrality, and mystifies police functions. (Manning sees this as the police's most powerful weapon in the public political arena, where funding and job security issues are decided.)
4. The police represent the political authorities' ability to maintain the status quo. This is an especially important theme in a diverse society because it means that social/ethnic groups will retain their relative position on the political-moral ladder. "By enforcing the law, [police] are always enforcing someone's interests against someone else's" (Manning, 1977, p. 6).
5. Police both symbolize the social order that is to be maintained and hold the capacity to stop citizens from committing acts that threaten that order.
6. The drama that is associated with police, mostly through informational public media portrayals of police—here, Manning gives the instance of a funeral for a slain officer—offers proof of the police presence and reaffirms the centrality of formal control in daily life.

In other work, Manning (1986, 1988) finds basic problems of policing in England and the United States to be endemic and structural, largely because the police system is a social organization that is not autonomous from its environment. For this reason, Manning says, all criticism of the functioning of police departments in these countries should consider the relevance of police theory to the everyday reality of policing. Manning's observations reveal that the police perceive their environment as a threat. They are legally justified to use violence, authority, and aggression as required in acts of law enforcement, but they are subject to varying public definitions of acceptable police intervention. They have developed strategies and techniques to deal with differing aspects of the threatening environment. These devices usually dramatize the image of police as being effective and in control.

The concerns of this study are refractions of Manning's observations. Police officers have a sense of occasion and present themselves to the public generally in a manner designed to win confidence and to legitimate their authority. Such norms, however, are often interdicted by the exigencies of the event and the kind of people they encounter: For example, a teenager mouths off and a cop "loses it." Likewise, mediated representations of cops can offer a competing standard by which the street officer is judged. If cops struggle to define themselves, through word and action, to the populace, they find themselves equally in a state of tension with the TV cop—that in one sense, the people are watching over the shoulder of the real one. How much is this duality appreciated by cops? How does it affect their presentation? How does it affect the way they view reactions by their audience, the public? How does it help push some activities from the front stage to the back stage? Does it affect the content and character of back-stage discussions and behavior? In essence, we can ask whether street cops, at least those encountered in this study, see themselves as antagonists or extensions of the culture's stereotype of the police officer.

Another study that has contributed to understanding police work was conducted of the Amsterdam police department by Maurice Punch (1979). Punch's follow-up studies (1985, 1986) were able to sort and sift prior conclusions, often finding that his first impressions were wrong. This in itself is an important cautionary tale for ethnographers who tend not to repeat their field excursions. His first informal meetings with police, as an instructor at a British university where a number of police officers studied, introduced Punch to the public and private worlds of policing. As one officer told him, "One thing you have to understand is that when you join the police you have to learn to break the law" (Punch, 1985, p. 209). This view was also prevalent in literature on American policing and was fixed in his mind as Punch gained access to and began the first of three studies on the Amsterdam police.

Nevertheless, he reports being "struck" by the absence of deviance in his first effort, from 1974 to 1976, during an observational study of patrol work in the inner-city district. Punch found, only after the completion of his study, that some of his key informants had been less than honest with him on the topic of police corruption. In a conversation after an evening's drinking, two of his informants demanded,

> How much do you think you found out when you were with us? You wrote some-where that you thought we were openhearted. Well, we only let you see what we wanted you to see. You only saw about fifty percent. We showed you only half of the story. (Punch, 1979, p. 13)

Punch suggests that no matter how certain the participant observer is of getting the "whole story," there may be another world behind the scenes that she or he is never allowed to witness.

This is the back stage of dramaturgy to be defined more clearly and explored more extensively later. However, a typical justification of the ethnographic research method is that it and its applicant can enter the back stage, which may be inaccessible to all other forms of research. For the back stage is not simply a place where hidden events transpire or where people say "what they really think." It is a context, largely only observable and in earshot of those who are invited to be there. A participant-observer who has gained the trust of the natives may be allowed to witness and hear what goes on. At the same time, as Punch implies by his follow-up experience and the revelation of the officers, there are back stages and there are *back* stages. There may very well be an inner sanctum that an ethnographer never penetrates. This may be simply the true thoughts of the subject but also might be a conversation topic that is never voiced or shared with outsiders. The ethnographer can never really know what she or he is missing. We can only hope that the evidence we do hear and see— and, in my case, photograph as well—is an approximation of certain truths about the subjects. If we are not deceived, we can translate the life, work, and ideas of the studied culture so that it can be understood by an audience that was never there. Furthermore, those who live the experience might approve, if not of the ethnography's interpretations, then of its data.

The secrecy of police may well stem from reasons beyond hiding deviant activities. Corruption and physical brutality are the most common behaviors outsiders (and the system itself) classify as deviant. Yet much more common and unseen or heard by the public are the back-stage activities of rough talk and making fun of the "customers"—the public. As will be discussed later, this was the case in the present ethnography—the deviance this observer encountered in cops was largely verbal, not physical. Cops sometimes engaged in discourse that they recognized would not create a good impression if seen or heard by the public or their superiors: cracking jokes about the citizenry, expressing moral judgments, complaining about superiors, goofing off, and so on. That these are deviant acts by public standards (although they are common to all professions) does not make them deviant by street standards; it simply relegates them routinely to the back stage, certainly out of earshot of superiors and the press.

That such a back stage must exist for cops is inevitable. Police are both regarded as essential and routinely condemned for their failures and inadequacies. Reform of police organizations has been and continues to be attempted—hiring more and better cops (highly educated, from diverse backgrounds), increasing monetary resources, professionalizing the occupation—but has resulted in little change in the level of public satisfaction. Police do not see their role as simply comparing behavior to a clear legal standard and either making or not making an arrest. For a variety of reasons—the law is ambiguous, the parties concerned wish the officer(s) to "do something" but do not want an arrest as resolution, offended parties will not sign a complaint, the officer(s) were not present when the misdemeanor took place, neither of the parties concerned are blameless, and so on—arrest is very often not the way to maintain order. Indeed, as one cop put it to me, *PP:* "People accuse us of being subjective and selective about arrests, but if we arrested everyone who broke the law, no one would be left outside of jail."

A study by Richard Harris (1978) elucidates the background of the development of street cop culture. Harris attended a police academy and observed both recruits and training staff. Some of the most important training that goes on in the academy is behind the scenes, what Harris calls "out of sight" (i.e., the back stage). It is here that a personalized morality and a masculine ethos begin to develop, a general spirit influencing the "team stance" or "line" (in Goffman's terminology) of the organization. Harris notes the importance of the police academy not only for training recruits but in the sustaining and stabilizing of the entire police organization. He asserts that many have dismissed the police academy as being irrelevant and inconsequential, coinciding with the police's own view that training in the academy is out of step with the demands of everyday police work and that real training occurs on the job. His own observations suggest that the work and training taking place at the police academy could not be so easily eliminated. The academy has some subjective meaning that is likely to influence later roles of policing chosen by patrolmen.

John Van Maanen (1978b), in another study, also analyzed the police academy, then followed recruits and their socialization process into the patrol division. He found that the academy readied recruits to accept the views of police work held and transmitted by the police squad; it did not, however, reveal the precise definition of police work. This instruction was given at the level of everyday policing, verbally and by example. Veteran cops are both supportive and wary of the "rookie," extending him more and more good will as the rookie proves his ability to act wisely and from proper motivation. Veterans bring the rookie into line and warn him through words and actions of the "mean and dark spirits out to get him," both on the street and in the department, should he fail to behave according to the fundamentals of police culture. Rookie socialization is highly dependent on his repertoire of experiences as narrated primarily by his field training officer (FTO) but also by fellow patrolmen working in the same precinct and on the same shift. This means that socialization to police culture is a highly local process. It is also an ongoing endeavor; cops go to "school" with each new experience. Van Maanen's findings that socialization of the police recruit takes the path of least resistance, where the rookie becomes "similar in sentiment and behavior to his peers" (p. 306), suggest that attempts to professionalize or otherwise change police culture are likely to fail.

Relatively uniquely situated in context is the research by Paul Shadgett (1990), a Toronto police officer who undertook an observational study of his own colleagues. Shadgett's study stresses the inordinate amount of time that police spend in the service of other institutions, accounting and preparing for their work. No other ethnographic exploration has as clearly emphasized the mounds of paperwork that confront the officer in the line of duty. In his view, police do very little crime work and joke about it openly: "Well, I'm gonna go out and fight crime." Shadgett accurately describes the make-work drudgery that accompanies being a police officer. For example, a 1-hour investigation of an injury due to an auto accident involving a driver under the influence of alcohol required the filing of 16 reports.

Finally, adding another cross-cultural context to the view of the dilemmas of police work is Marc Jeanjean's (1990) *Ethnologie Chez les Policiers,* an account of his 2 years of participant observation in a police department in a middle-class *arrondissement* of Paris. In some ways, his study is a necessary comparative to conclusions about police work in North America and England, for the French police are in essence a national police, much more regimentized, organized, and centralized than police in the United States, Canada, or England. Jeanjean's findings, however, are very much like those previously cited. In fact, it is testament that perhaps all Western peoples, at least, make similar demands of their "constables on patrol," despite variations in the system of justice or the national culture. In Paris, Jeanjean reports, the uniformed street officers (*la tenue*) who make up the bulk of the force also undergo negotiations of status between their "clients" and superiors, as well as many other bureaucratic and social agencies that control French life. Jeanjean emphasizes the tedium of the work of *la tenue,* barely giving any space in his research to what would constitute appropriate fare for a television program about cops here or in France. They, too, serve largely as *gardiens de la paix,* often breaking, bending, or subjectively interpreting the law to attempt to render justice and restore order. The mean-world phenomenon, the suspicion cops have of people they meet, is also underscored, especially on urban night shifts, where few honest citizens occupy the demimonde. Revealingly, the French cops also saw themselves as negotiating a public stereotype influenced by American television. One officer complained, "Starsky and Hutch have done more to hurt the profession than anything else." In contrast, real police work is slogging and monotonous. Finally, *la tenue* are also quite sensitive to public criticism and feel to some extent that they are asked to achieve an impossible task in a society that is increasingly breaking down, no longer responding to the official and approved methods of law enforcement.

The view of policing, particularly of street policing, which emerges through ethnographic study, reveals several consistent observations.

1. Police show an awareness of being in a "no-win" situation. Crime sociologist James Q. Wilson (1968) has argued, in line with previous work cited above, that

> in managing conflict, his [the patrolman's] task is to maintain order under circumstances such that the participants and the observer are likely to disagree as to what constitutes a reasonable and fair settlement and he is likely to be aware of hostility, alert to the possibility of violence, and uncertain that the authority symbolized by his badge and uniform will be sufficient for him to take control of the situation. (p. 278)

As they attempt to maintain order and enforce the law in a heterogeneous capitalist society, police recognize that they are revered as heroes while being almost simultaneously cursed as either oppressive authoritarians or inept buffoons.

2. Police perceive a loss of status—a decrease in autonomy and ability to exercise discretion on the job.

3. Police, at all levels, are concerned with their public image, negotiating encounters with government leaders and citizens on the basis of the image they think others have of police in general and of detectives and street cops in particular. This has led the police organization to employ a formal, statistical evaluation of policing effectiveness. For the cop on the street, image maintenance requirements quite often determine the choice of an appropriate policing role, social attitude, and public behavior.

4. Whatever divisions of race, class, and gender among police officers, whatever cliques of friendship or acquaintance may develop among officers of the same rank and duties, the cop is still a cop, and reaction to him and his reaction to others are tempered by the visible and literal uniformity of appearance. Cops are highly susceptible to viewing the world in an us-versus-them dichotomy. It is almost inescapable in the mean world of policing not to think of everyone who is not a cop as a potential danger. This, above all other things, increases group solidarity but also commensurably heightens group sensitivity to stereotypical portrayal, especially that arising from outside sources. In this study, I consider the mass media as one of those sources.

5. Although it may be heuristically useful to say that cops are sometimes "on"—that is, they adopt their street persona—and "off" when they relax into their true character, in real life there are varying degrees of both conditions.

Cops understand that the role they play is a negotiation, although one that may be forcefully activated between themselves, their superiors, the legal system and all its helpful and hurtful representatives, and the public, including the bad guys. Autonomy for an officer is, to some extent, control of what personas he adopts in what situations and how much he feels that the persona is the result of his own independent choice and not forced on him by those outside sources.

5

Front Stage and Back Stage

The stage is a lived metaphor. Flesh-and-blood cops are "real" in the sense that they exist outside of the diegesis of a television set or a cinema screen. But they are also, in many ways, performers concerned about their star status, the flow of the script, remembering their lines, and many other dramaturgically analogous manifestations. Even before the current emphasis on "community policing," a study found that "72 percent of a policeman's work day is spent in some form of communication activity" (Erikson, Cheatham, & Haggard, 1976, p. 299). My purpose in this chapter is to describe the dimensions and the ramifications of the process of communication with the cop as performer. In particular, these observations are divided into the performances of the front stage, that is, for public consumption, and the back stage, for private or in-group (team) consumption. I will not attempt to connect every aspect of the cops' words, gestures, and behavior to mass-mediated norms and forms; rather, the cops' performance should be considered a baseline for our (and, I believe, their) explorations of the contrasts to mass-mediated cops.

Deeming a cop an "actor" on a "stage" is not to transform him into either a schemer declaiming clichés to the third balcony or a marionette of some unseen director. As Turner (1986) noted in defending his concept of social drama, "The drama *is* rooted in social reality, not imposed on it" (p. 37). To call a cop a performer does not negate the objective conditions of his existence; rather, it accounts for an important way that the cop negotiates his status at work, in public, and among his fellows. As Turner further defines the task,

If man is a sapient animal, a tool making animal, a self making animal, a symbol using animal, he is, no less, a performing animal, *Homo performans,* not in the sense, perhaps, that a circus animal may be a performing animal, but in the sense that man is a self-performing animal—his performances are, in a way, *reflexive,* in performing he reveals himself to himself. (p. 37)

Figure 5.1.

In this view, the theatrical conveyance not only challenges the police officer to speak and act in certain fashions with considerable circumspection but also allows him to organize and regulate his orientation toward his profession. In particular, the performance is driven by the hopes and fears of the cop and his audience; these emotive expectations obviously arise from somewhere, and it is clear that cops assume mass-mediated representations of police work and criminality, both "real" and "fictional," to be a primary influence in how people react to them personally as performers. The police officer is a "star" trying to gain creative control over the course of an often-unpredictable drama, but others, from superiors to the public, may accede to or challenge his purposes and precepts. Although in most social dramas in other professions, bending others to one's will, forcing people to comply, and physically dominating others are metaphors, for cops it is articulated reality (see Figure 5.1). In the equation, however, as we shall see in later chapters, mass media jostle the stage, skew the script, and upset the characterizations; if not an actual enemy, they are a rival definer and shaper of the narrative that street cops live.

THE FRONT STAGE

It is a common assumption of stage and screen that a star must compose his or her roles from his or her intrinsic character. Thus, Edgar G. Robinson was viewed with terror by hotel clerks expecting a gangster's temper, and soap opera villainesses are assaulted in supermarkets by irate viewers wishing to avenge televisual transgressions. For the cop, such a divergence between the stage life and the civilian life, between persona and person, appears negligible for those who are there to observe it. At the end of the shift, officers go to their lockers and remove their uniforms; in fact, most just change their shirts or go home in an undershirt.[1] In addition, they strip off their symbols and instruments of office, from the silver badge to the Sam Browne belt and all its accessories, including flashlight, key case, mace, baton, handcuffs (two pairs), hygiene gloves, radio, and gun and holster. With this simple ritual, a cop becomes a civilian—but he does not change his basic character. The gruff, taciturn cop remains dour at the bar after work; the easygoing jokester starts up his home improvement projects in the same genial spirit; the sober family man is just as steady in the squad as picking up groceries at the market. In the time I spent with a few of the cops off-duty as friends or acquaintances, I observed no Superman/Clark Kent shift of character from *gardien de la paix* to milquetoast.

The disjuncture in terms of public reaction, however, is sharp. The wearing of a police uniform transforms an ordinary person into something else, from an anonymous face in the crowd to a "cop," facing all the prejudices and stereo-types that the public may have accumulated about the profession. Cops them-selves comment on this separation: *PP:* "People don't recognize you with your uniform off." I experienced this phenomenon personally. At a late-night car stop, a man shouted in anger at the cop and then turned to me, the lowly reserve, and unleashed a blistering complaint about cops who had "nothing better to do" than persecute him. Three days later, I saw the man as he rolled a shopping cart down the aisle at Target. Our eyes locked, but I detected no sign of recogni-tion in his expression; I was grateful that this is so. Cops also appreciate the off-duty anonymity. To be in uniform in public, however, is to be in the front stage. Its exact location and type of audience vary, but cops are always aware that *someone* may be looking at them practically everywhere they go in uniform.

The Public Eye

The distinction between front and back stage is not necessarily geographic. The front stage can exist in police stations when visitors or suspects are present or in the squad car when on an open street. The booking procedure, for exam-ple, takes place within the station, behind concrete walls and steel doors, yet others—aside from the visual ethnographer—may be watching. People pass-ing outside may witness the goings-on through the window. In the new jail, which was constructed during my tenure at the St. Louis Park Police Depart-ment (SLP-PD), a video camera connected to the dispatcher's office records the proceedings in the main booking room and each jail cell (excluding the corner that contains the toilet). The station is hardly a fortress of solitude for uniformed street cops. There are superiors—the captain and the chief—about during the day hours and sometimes at night. On each shift there are sergeants and, again more so in the day, the secretarial and clerical staff, the cleaning staff, and assorted contract workers. Dispatchers, community service officers, Explorers, and even the occasional ride-along may also be around a corner or in a bathroom stall. In addition, people stop by to pick up a form, talk to an officer, or ask a question. Typically they are handled at the front desk, but they are still in earshot and, if they are brought further in, are in eye view as well. Some civilians (e.g., those coming by to talk to a detective or take custody of a juvenile) may enter the inner areas of the station. Finally, group tours are conducted for the public and for relatives of employees. In short, even in the back stage of the police station, the cop is never certain of being alone and completely out of sight or hearing of the "not-we," including the public or the quasi-public and superiors (Ericson, 1994a, pp. 168-169; 1994b, pp. 134-136).

That they are being observed at all is one measure of how cops inhabit the front stage as perhaps no other member of society. Is it a contradiction that in a normal street situation—where cops are neither undercover nor want to surreptitiously observe the behavior of others—they want to be noticed, yet feel some discomfort at being scrutinized? The issue of exactly how and how much people look at cops is complex and the flip side of being a "star"—as it is for actual movie and television performers. Objectively, a police officer can point to the rubberneck phenomenon that always occurs around the car stop. Cars slow down when passing a cop writing up a ticket by the side of the road. Officers have remarked to me, and I have either absorbed or independently observed, "People tend to look at us," or "They stare at us like we're from Mars" or "like we have bolts sticking out of our heads." Many times on ride-alongs, I would turn around and see someone at an intersection, stopped, or even driving by, staring.

I conducted an informal experiment in the squad car on two daytime shifts to try to obtain some estimate of the quantity and quality of passing attention paid to cops. I kept a notebook on my lap as we drove around; looking out the passenger window as other cars stopped or drove by, I would check off each vehicle, its number of passengers, and a brief notation of whether they looked at us. It was truly an unscientific exercise. Calls, conversations with the officer, and other distractions did not make my observations of the public consistent or comprehensive, nor did I note the quality or length of the engagement, people staring a long time versus casually glancing. Neither did I note the difference between when we were driving in traffic and when we were stopped at a light. According to this rough inquiry, however, in more than 80% of the cars that passed by us, at least one person took a look at me in uniform on the passenger side of the car. If this does not prove that cops are always being watched, it does suggest that they might have considerable fodder for retaining the perception that they are being watched. Perhaps more important, even if they do not notice, they must consider the *possibility* that they might be watched.

Small incidents suggest the paradox of this level of scrutiny. I sat with a cop in a parking lot where he had stopped to catch up on his paperwork. Another cop drove up, parallel, but from the opposing direction, so that the drivers faced each other, the typical cop conversation vehicle deployment. They talked; I joined in sometimes. They discussed what happened last shift ("that guy scored a 2.1 on the machine" [Breathalyzer]), how far behind they were on their paperwork, and problems in remodeling a kitchen at home. It was a quiet weekend afternoon; few calls crackled over the radio. Then a dispatcher informed one of cops (on his cell phone) that a woman in a nearby apartment building had complained about these two cops parking their squads there for such a long time. After a few minutes, the two cars pulled out. The cop I was riding with did not use any expletives but emphatically told me what he thought of that "busybody." He added, "Unless we're kicking down doors, people think we aren't working."

The awareness that observation is possible or even probable, that the public is watching, is omnipresent. This was illustrated to me on one late-night ride. The department rotated in three shifts during most my tenure with the SLP police. The shift I most often traveled on (about 60% of the time) was the 4 to 11 p.m. shift, but sometimes I would ride along for at least the first part of the dog shift, 11 p.m. to 6 or 7 a.m. Because I worked during the day as well, these would be the only times that the ethnography could be pursued. It did mean, however, that, unlike cops, who might adjust their sleep patterns during the 6 or 7 months on a particular shift, I was permanently changing my waking and sleeping hours. Often, by 3 or 4 a.m., I would be near comatose and simply ask the cop to drop me at the station, from which point I would go home. Occasionally, in my enthusiasm to stick it out, I would fail to recognize how tired I really was. One night, the cop with whom I was riding pulled up at the station and said, "I think it's time for you to go home and go to bed." When I asked him why, he said, "Well, you're falling asleep, and it's pretty embarrassing when people see a cop falling asleep in the cruiser." It was true: I was wearing my reserve uniform. In my notes, scrawled just after stumbling in my front door, I wrote "most embarrassing moment of my ethnography."

I rode along several nights later, when the incident seemed to have been forgotten. But then we stopped at a local hotel that put out coffee and desserts for the late-shift officers of several neighboring cities. Mostly the officers drop in and out, but if it is a very slow night, as many as eight or nine may congregate. This practice is not officially sanctioned, but on dead nights it is no breach of honor. Conversations were light: what had happened that day, house repairs, health problems, and a little shop gossip. Then one cop from another city yawned and said he should just park his squad and catch up on sleep. My cop cheerfully announced, "Dave here just does it while we ride around." I don't recall saying anything; I do recall being chagrined. The topic resurfaced once in a while in the months to come, always with humor, but the issue is nevertheless a serious one: A cop can afford to look mean, brutal, or callous but not ridiculous. Even at 4 a.m., a uniformed cop in a squad car is on the front stage.

Time Spent on the Front Stage

Time is also a factor in the police officer's star status. The cop's performance of his or her duty is not open-ended. As previously mentioned, the entire city of SLP would often be served by no more than four or five officers in squads, on patrol. There is a premium placed, individually and departmentally, on the rapid resolution of any situation, within the bounds of caution. The motorist delayed from some important task, as they all seem to be, by a cop who catches him speeding does not understand the passage of such time, although his own time is of course precious. The minutes he waits for the police officer to fill out the requisite forms and check his driver information are stretched into a seeming eternity. But likewise, people quarreling at the scene of an incident, clamoring, "I said this, he said that, she said something else" can also make the police officer feel that his time is being wasted needlessly. Even if he has no place else to go, he still must be available on patrol in case a call comes in. Hence, as a star, he cannot hold back and simply wait for events to develop. Like a star, he must propel the plot and try to bend the storyline to his will. Of course, in most situations in which people want and need a police officer, the dramatic actions he takes are exactly what they wish for.

This is one of the discordances with televisual reality, which is marked by its compactness. Even in continuing drama series, there must be some minor denouement at the end of each episode. Twenty-three minutes in the half-hour program and 43 minutes in the 1-hour program are accorded to the story itself. But merely the fact that mediated representations of cops have a built-in time limit whereas extramedia reality has its own form of time constraint (often without a three-act structure) does not mean that the time factor is encoded or decoded similarly by the viewing audience in the former case and the cop performer and his public in the latter. The televisual narrative is absolutely governed by a preset chronology. Not since the early days of television has a dramatic series been able to spill over from its time slot. A viewer flipping through *TV Guide* can ascertain without any uncertainty that *Law & Order* will be on from 9 to 10 p.m. Only major breaking news, sports programs, or weather emergencies will interrupt or occlude the program's appearance. There is indisputably a comfort factor involved here, part of the enacting and relieving of tension that television provides. We know, in an episodic series, that 2 or 3 minutes before the hour all loose ends will be tied up and all criminals will be punished or, infrequently, let off the hook. Time is a signal for closure on television.

In street reality, this is not the case. Cops are under compunction to finish the job at hand, barring emergency, before beginning a new one. This is in some sense like television, but it was rare that the full paperwork and machineries of closure were enacted during the time accorded to one incident. A cop taking a burglary report, for example, will write it up on the scene but will probably complete it later. An arrest narrative may not be written until the next day. The explanation for what has happened, the enacting of bureaucratic closure from the point of view of the street officer, is not necessarily temporally connected to the incident itself, or it may be only partly connected. Sometimes back in the squad car the cop jots down some quick notes on his pad to help him write his narrative later.

In another sense, there is a contrariety between the time factor on TV and on the street: Although the constraint on how much time a police officer can allot to any individual incident is reasonably pressing, it is also relative to the situation and to the context of the shift. As we might imagine, the less serious the crime, the less time a cop may feel is worth expending on it. But more important, a cop will have a feel for the night (e.g., "It's a busy night; let's get this over with."). A Friday night when there are many car stops, loud party calls, and assaults puts a premium on each man-hour of the department. Likewise, a cop is aware of how many of the other squads are on call. "Well, Dave, we're patrolling the city alone tonight," or "Everybody else is on call. I better try and stay free," or "Even the sergeants are out tonight—it's busy." Again, that a cop's street existence can have rhythms of frenzy and slackness is itself a major divergence from TV world, where entire episodes devoted to slack time would be unthinkable.

Observations of such contrasts were made in the squad car: "They won't film *Cops* here tonight." There was some predictability about which nights would be busier than others—Saturdays more than Tuesdays, for example. Particular times of day had some level of relative frequency of calls as well, such as rush hour versus 4 a.m. But even though SLP is a border suburb of Minneapolis and has its share of crime, the cops maintained that "we're not Eden Prairie," an outer suburb with a reputation for even less criminal activity. Still, there were long nights. The bitter winter, which the cops speculated was one of the reasons that Minnesota had a relatively low crime rate, brought about dead spells that could last entire shifts. One Tuesday afternoon/night shift—New Year's Day, in fact—we had only one call, a barking dog. The officer cited *Cops* and *Hill Street Blues* and even once mockingly called into his radio, "Car 54, where are you?" This lull should not have been an issue to me, the ethnographer; after all, we had some good conversations about police work, and a slow night should have produced no fewer data than a staccato of calls would have on a busy night. But, as noted previously, I would often get caught up in the torpor myself, thinking, "I wish something would happen. About time for a call. . . ."

Finally, a crucial distinction between time on TV and time on the front stage of the street is the relative weight of importance of an incident. On TV, everything is important; indeed, the old maxim of the dramatic plot is that nothing should be included that does not contribute to its progression. The precious moments of a television program are expended on scenes and situations that are deemed attractive to an audience and relevant to the narrative of the show. If characters on a TV show waste time, that wasting of time—for example, cops on stakeout ultimately frustrated by the suspect never showing—is in itself crucial to the propelling of the story, the drawing of a character, or the constructing of an atmosphere. Street police work, on the other hand, is a myriad of irrelevancies. There is a call to a location; it is a barking dog complaint, now usually handled by a community officer rather than a patroller, but the patroller may answer the summons. There is no dog barking when the cop arrives, and no one answers the door at the house, so no action is taken. Later, someone complains about a suspicious car driving up and down the street. We arrive, only to find no car. The report: GOA, Gone on Arrival. There is no connection here with the greater narrative of the day of the life of the cop. The time seems wasted, but the duty is essential; someone has to respond when the public dials 911. Thus, street cops are not always held to a dramatic narrative, even if they sometimes judge themselves by one.

THE BACK STAGE

The back stage can best be described as related to the *content* of conversation rather than locale. In this vein, it is useful to identify the back stage's relation to what James Scott (1990) has called the hidden transcript: discourse not meant to be publicly uttered or printed. Scott argues that much of what passes for history ignores what is said off the record:

> Every subordinate group creates, out of its ordeal, a "hidden transcript" that represents the critique of power spoken behind the back of the dominant. The powerful, for their part, also create a hidden transcript, representing the practice and claims of their rule that cannot be openly avowed. (p. xii)

Hidden sentiments, expressed in hidden transcripts, are not just dark murmurings of rebellion against a liege lord; they can also be tools of social cohesion and stability. The hidden transcripts of police officers—who have power over the public but also recognize that the public (and superiors) hold power over them—ultimately serve such a purpose, though at times in their extremes they may seem dysfunctional.

In my study, cops would occasionally joke about my presence "coming back to haunt them" (i.e., "When you publish this, Dave, try not to make me look like a jerk."). Sometimes their behavior is an example in itself, a cautionary presentation or face presented for the observer. As example: Late one shift, two cops sorted through beer and marijuana paraphernalia that they had confiscated from a teen "kegger." One of them joked, *PP:* "Here, Dave, take our picture. Now you'll really have something on us." One officer pretended to be smoking a bong, and another feigned drinking from a can of beer. All of this took place in the middle of the station. I obliged them and took the picture with my 24-mm lens, to get the contexts of the secretaries' desks and captain's office door. The second officer adjusted the gun in his holster, grimaced, and with Dirty Harry emphasis said, "If that ever sees the light of day, I'll kill you."

The hidden transcripts of the back stage fall into categories of speech and behaviors. The first of these are the feelings, attitudes, and assumptions officers express about their fellow officers. The second category covers carping about the job itself and criticism of other colleagues. This includes police officers' opinions of their superiors in rank: sergeants, lieutenants, the captain, the police chief, and even city hall. But complaint may also go down the ladder toward those people within the police organization whom officers believe to be below them, such as reserves, dispatchers, and even rookie officers. Third, there are negative back-stage appraisals of the public, the citizenry. These often consist of either moral judgments or exasperation at people's "stupidity," a less harsh term than it sounds.

Each of these covert actions and hidden transcripts exists in a state of tension and release. They are of the back stage, usually enacted not in the public arena in front of citizens or in court but in small groups of two or three officers eating lunch or chatting briefly at an incident scene or between parked police cars. At the same time, in moments of social collapse or great pressure, hidden transcripts can erupt into extremely vocal public episodes. A police officer stoically enduring the excuses from a lady as to why she had to park her Mercedes in a fire zone would normally respond with his own dry lecture on how the law should not make exceptions and would give the woman a ticket, saving his ire for release in the car. In this case, though, it had been a very long, trying day, so the cop cut the woman's expostulations off and told her to shut up and "stop acting like a walking stereotype."

Likewise, good-natured ribbing in roll call can escalate to a bitter outright complaint against the perceived indolence of one of the sergeants, the rudeness in an officer's voice when he speaks to his dispatcher over the police airwaves is so apparent that a lieutenant reprimands him for it, and so on. The extraordinary thing about hidden transcripts is how they are able to remain hidden. Of course, "hidden" does not mean that only those who "hide" them are aware of them. A cop can be acutely aware of his own unpopularity and the flaws of ability and character many of the other officers believe he holds, even if 99% of what is said about him is behind his back. Part of this knowledge arises from the intimacy of the group: As family members learn to read each other's mood by a nuance of expression or voice, so too do those in the small police department. It is part of the drama of cop work that many hidden transcripts within the team of officers are in fact secret from no one in the team at all.

The ironic contrast to the mass-mediated cop, at least in fiction, is an object of comment. On TV, there are no hidden transcripts, or at least there are none by the end of an episode. In fact, the viewer is given omniscient access to private conversations and deeds; the voyeurism of the medium allows us to see and hear what is "really going on." "TV cops, they have no privacy," notes one officer. Because they don't, of course, the supposed authenticity of the events is heightened—it must be more real because we see it from the inside. Yet the transparency of the motivations and ideas of TV cops and crooks is simply a code signifying realism, not an actual insight.

Talking About Colleagues

One particular incident provoked back-stage discourse on the obligations of colleagues. Ray, an officer with whom I was riding, was called to an apartment building where the sounds of a domestic dispute were reported. As is typical, another officer was called for backup. Ray and I arrived first and went up to the second floor. Ray stopped outside the apartment door and listened. We could hear people talking inside, but it did not clearly sound like a fight. Meanwhile, the other officer arrived downstairs in his squad car. He radioed up, asking our status. Ray was irritated by this and walked away from the door. He waited what seemed an eternity of 5 seconds before answering that everything was okay. He stood there, his hand on the radio, midway between the exit and the apartment, contemplating a decision. As usual, I said nothing. Finally, Ray shook his head with great emphasis, and we walked back in silence to the car. The other officer had already left. For the next half hour or so, driving around, Ray told me how "un-fucking-believable" it was that "that lazy fat-ass had radioed for his status instead of coming up" to join him, to back him up. I gathered from the vitriol that this had not been the first time that this had happened and that he perceived that the other officer was unenthusiastic in his backing up on calls.

Unlike most police incidents, this had a relative resolution. When we went to lunch, we ran into the other officer. Ray made a sarcastic comment, something like, "Thanks for the backup." The other officer at first shrugged it off but then said that he did not think he needed to come upstairs at the scene. Both men dropped the line of argument; I never saw any evidence of further tension between them. The situation did not recur, and Ray never brought it up again. I never asked him, so I do not know whether the subject was permanently dropped or if it was the kind of recurring tension that always exists because of the danger of the work and the reliance on trust of fellow officers. It seemed an example of an aggrievement once aired then dissipated. Perhaps the violation of the code was never repeated, and thus the irritation that Ray felt was not stoked by further incidents. This is an instance in which the expression of what was at first a hidden transcript, a monologue given by Ray in my presence, was then released to a wider audience, the offending officer and a few others in the lunchroom. It would be inconceivable, though, at least on the basis of the observations I made, for a complaint about a fellow officer's conduct to be aired publicly on a street with civilian eyewitnesses.

Another factor is that, with intracop talk, it is sometimes difficult to distinguish between jesting and real antipathy. I have often sat in the squad room while cops kidded each other to the point where an outsider walking in would assume that this was a roomful of enemies, with officers making exchanges, for example, such as, "Fuck you." "No, fuck *you*!" In one memorable incident, the taunting escalated until several of the officers drew guns on each other in a "Mexican stand-off." One completed the allusion by whistling the theme tune of *The Good, the Bad, and the Ugly*. I could not refrain from joining in the moment, so I set up to take a picture of them as they stood, guns frozen, pointed at each other. I said, "Wait, wait, wait. Okay, I'm ready. Fire!" The lead officer calmed the situation by proposing that they all shoot me instead, a suggestion that was met with general enthusiasm. This incident, and how it "played out," demonstrates the mixture of humor and toughness that is intrinsic to a working-class, male-dominated group. As one cop put it, "Having the other guys to joke around with 'makes the job.' "[2]

Talking About Superiors/Complaining About Work

Complaining about the work situation or superiors is endemic to any company or occupation. I did not find street cops more likely to whine than were the communication graduate students who were my cohort at the time of the ethnography or junior professors at the time of this writing. As in those work experiences, criticism of fellow officers (people of the same rank) is almost never shared with superiors. On the other hand, criticism of superiors is freely shared among all officers. As example, one new department policy at the time of my ethnography—the community policing initiative—was singled out for generally negative critique by officers. There is an antipathy among street cops for feel-good rhetoric and actions; this was manifest in ideas and expressions about community policing. Community policing is defined differently wherever it is put into practice, but in SLP, it meant generally more attempts to involve neighborhood groups in advising and cooperating with the police department, implementing or expanding programs such as DARE (Drug Abuse Resistance Education), or assigning officers to the public schools.

"Cops don't like new things," said one officer, and perhaps the suspicion of reform is based on the recollections that last year's reforms may be this year's hoary bureaucracies. The specific objection to community policing was a reasonable one: The more man-hours allocated to nontraditional activities, the thinner the blue line on the street. This was an unresolved collision of worldviews between the hierarchy of the department, especially the chief, and a majority of the street officers. The department maintained that they were not losing any street time; officers felt that they were.

In any case, the specific target of the complaining was less important for our purposes than its rationale. Here the officers are defining cop work as street time: in the squad, patrolling, answering calls, stopping cars, or, occasionally, uncovering crimes in progress. Such a definition of cop work fits perfectly with the idea that cops are "there," which means wearing the uniform, driving the car, carrying the gun, and doing the duty. Other mandated behaviors such as speaking to community groups seem less like real police work by this categorization scheme. In this fashion, cops create a hierarchy of values on what is authentically who they are and what they do. They are not social workers, public relations operatives, or hand-holders; they are cops. It is part of their struggle to maintain autonomy in the work to indicate disapproval—largely through criticism, sometimes hidden, sometimes directly expressed through, for example, union motions—and to put boundaries on what the work entails. Community policing is not seen as inherently unsound, but any challenge that seems to shift cops away from the role they comfortably use as their definition of group and of self is understandably viewed with suspicion.

Yet, all street cops have routinized limits on their autonomy. These in turn may be recognized and accepted, chafed at and critiqued, or ignored. With every arrest, for example, an incident report must be filed, technically almost immediately. Because of the busy nature of certain shifts, though, officers might put off this task for several days. A measure of autonomy, however, can be a tool that management uses to reward officers who are cooperative; its withdrawal can act to punish those who are "troublemakers." One officer I rode with had been quite active in the union in filing several protests about department policies. He described himself to me as "making trouble for the administration." Being a member of the union, he had not actually been reprimanded or punished, but he did feel that he was being scrutinized more closely than other officers were. He told me that his reports were read more carefully and evaluated more stringently, his decisions were questioned more often, and so on.

When I asked him how this changed his work as a cop, that is, his street behavior—on the front stage—he stated, "When you're on their shit list they micromanage you, and you don't want to get too aggressive." By aggressive, he went on to explain, he meant that in situations in which one could follow one's instinct or go by the book, take a risk, or play it safe, he felt under great pressure to make whatever decision would be least likely to be questioned afterwards. He said he felt that this did not make him a worse cop, but that micromanaging, in the long run, did reduce his effectiveness and make him less likely to go and "sniff out" crime. He shrugged, "That's the way they want it." He did not bemoan this difficulty; that would have been seen as a sign of weakness to other cops or to myself. He did speculate that "they wouldn't mind if he quit," but he had no intention of doing so.

Interestingly, I came to believe that he was wrong about his own imposed reserve. Perhaps it is a relative judgment and that years before, when he was not on the "shit list," he must have been a really aggressive cop. Of all the officers I rode with, he was the one who seemed to me to take the most risks, was the most aggressive, and was the most interested in quickly taking charge in a situation. For example, he was very unlikely to call a backup in situations in which I think many other cops would have—a late-night car stop, where several young males sat in a junker car, or at house alarm calls. Among the other cops, he also had a reputation for "getting out there" and sometimes of even being reckless. I never mentioned this to him, nor did I tell others of his perceptions of the department's attitudes or his own passivity (I never repeated what one cop said to me to another cop). So it was almost startling sometimes to ride with him and see how, in many ways, he was a walking stereotype of the tough, aggressive street cop, but yet in the two or three discussions we had on his philosophy of police work, he claimed to feel "handcuffed" by his situation in the department. It was less a case of cognitive dissonance than of relative position judgment.

In all, complaining about superiors in daily life, griping about the work, and whining about policies are rebellions but also "multivocal," that is, speaking to many aspects of the cop and his work (Turner, 1968, p. 17). These behaviors cannot then be interpreted as simply the cataloguing of peeves and grievances. Whether or not they serve the interests of the established order by giving the weak a sense of power that dilutes their incentive to seize real physical or political power depends on the situation. Reviling the "suits," the "brass," and the "pencil pushers" or criticizing departmental policy can be seen as a safety valve release rather than the first signs of mutiny. There is a certain complicit and illicit pleasure in ritually lowering the superior behind his back. Hidden transcripts may never empower peasants, cops, or graduate students, but they give one a sense of scoring points off the "oppressor." Complaining is not deviance—literally everybody does it—but it is a strategy of empowerment that may, in the end, serve both the employee and the organization (cf. Alicke et al., 1992; Kowalski, 1996).

Making Moral and Mental Judgments About the Public

Cops critique each other and their superiors but also the public, and those critiques tend to devolve into two categories. The first is the moral judgment. As suggested earlier, one way to parse the people with whom cops came into contact is between the "bad guys" and the "good guys." Like all boundaries in police work, such a moral judgment could be flexible: "That kid used to be a little shit but he's really turned around," or "I guess we were wrong about that guy. He's okay. His story checks out." But generally, moral judgments stick. The man whom cops feel sure to be a rapist rarely turns out to be a saint; the innocent gray-haired old lady is not, after all, a Moriarty in lace. When cops make moral judgments, they are often self-confirming because they are self-evident, and even those among us who may resist such judgments cannot help but believe the general nature of the appraisal to be correct.

The second type of judgment is of the stupidity of the public. People lie to cops; they are often stupid about how they lie. If people are stupid, that stupidity is again seemingly self-evident. "She was dumb to let the guy in the house," or "Can you believe it? The robber dropped his wallet on the pavement. What an idiot." Such judgments are well known in ethnographic literature, although they may appear in different guises. Manning (1986) suggests that because the police officer in face-to-face encounters is aiming to establish authority and exercise control, these situations are characteristically conflictual, a condition that stems also from a conflicted society and fosters distrust, lying, and secrecy. Citizens lie to the police, who have, in turn, come to expect them to do so. In line with such observations, I found that moral judgments and ascriptions of stupidity are not necessarily callously made or wantonly inflicted. They help cops make sense of their world and, to some extent, reward their own self-perceived acumen about human nature and foibles. In fact, the public's ignorance of police procedure or misguided assumptions about police work may actually assist the officer in the execution of his or her duty.

Van Maanen (1978c) has also written that the police create a social type and term (the "asshole") to account for people who do not accept the police definition of who is in charge of an encounter. He argues that identification and treatment of the asshole are "intimately related to the police production and represents an aspect of policing that is near the core of the patrolman's definition of his task" (p. 234). Labeling individuals as assholes distances police from their segmented audience. The asshole simplifies and orders the policeman's world, enabling him to classify others as like or unlike the asshole.

This classification scheme also provides a consensually approved (via police culture) means for remedying "out-of-kilter" situations that are seen as threats to police self-definition. Police self-definition is that of law enforcer, but their daily existence shows the police's primary role to be that of keeper of the peace. Labeling of asshole types often permits police to project law enforcement behavior—what police define as "real work" and what Van Maanen (1978c) refers to as "marginally legitimate arrests" of assholes—to otherwise peacekeeping situations. Van Maanen suggests that this is both expressive and a means of infusing ordinarily dull patrol work with a little excitement. He argues that the asshole serves as a "reified other," representing all persons whose actions attempt to control the police or that threaten their self-definition. Group cohesion is generated around the police's common relation to outsiders who disagree with the police line (see Becker, 1963).

In my encounters, people were sometimes called assholes (and a good deal worse), but most judgments concerned *immorality, stupidity,* and *lying.* Nevertheless, these verdicts fit Van Maanen's (1978c) descriptions of an attitude that provided a way for cops to make sense of their work and to provide entertainment. One example of a moral judgment and a "stupid" designation: a call from a woman in an upscale apartment building. She greeted us at the door in a bathrobe and bare feet. She started complaining the moment we entered the apartment in a loud, angry voice, like she wanted to have somebody at whom to yell and express her aggrievement and victimhood. She had been robbed, she told us, of her jewelry, TV set, and VCR. The cop began to take a report. What were the circumstances? It became tortuous and complicated. "I had a guest in my apartment last night." After 20 minutes of vagaries, the story came out. She met a guy at a bar the night before, they both got drunk, and she brought him home. When she woke up, he was gone, and so was her stuff. The cop was impassive. I think I detected a slight raised eyebrow when she said that she could not describe the thief except that he was "white and big." She added quickly, "I mean he was tall." At this point, the cop did press the inquiry slightly, but he avoided a sarcastic tone. "You can't give a more clear description?" Perhaps it was his polite inflection and the fact that he was still looking at the clipboard and form that she did not take this as an insult; she just said "no." Again and again, she made statements that begged for a sympathetic response, not one of "Well, that's just terrible that happened to you" but rather, "The bastard! How could he do that?" The cop made no comments other than those related to business. He gave her the usual line about the descriptions of the stolen merchandise being entered into the system and that they would call if it turned up. We left the apartment; the moment we were in the elevator, we turned to each other. The cop shook his head and released a snort. No words were needed to express his contempt for the woman's stupidity and recklessness.

Moral judgments are released into the front stage in situations in which they are less remonstration than methods of getting information or "doing good." In other words, moral judgment is part of the cop's tool kit. "Good" is most often at stake when children's welfare is in the balance. For example, I rode along with a female officer who accompanied a detective to make a follow-up visit on a complicated family situation. A woman's live-in boyfriend was arrested for molesting her daughter. He was ordered by the court to stay away from them, and the woman made a deal with child welfare authorities that she would not see him anymore and would report if he came by. She also promised to fully cooperate in his prosecution. The detective had learned that the boyfriend was living with them again, and they were planning to flee to Florida. At the apartment, the woman answered the door. We went in. The boyfriend was not inside, but there were packed suitcases, a man's clothing, big work boots, and various belongings in boxes—every sign unambiguously indicated that he had been here and they were planning to leave the city. The woman denied everything at first but then, as happens so often, after hearing seven or eight times "you're lying to us, aren't you?" she reversed course and admitted the truth.

At this point, the cop and the detective both pulled out moral judgment: "You have to choose between your boyfriend and your child." The woman started to cry. They pushed this line hard. She finally begged them to give her another chance. The next week, she was scheduled to give a deposition in the molestation case. Would she testify? She promised that she would. She said that when her daughter came home, they would go to her mother's house right away. The officers would return, wait for the boyfriend to come home, and arrest him for violating the court order. The moral judgment, accompanied with the implied threat to take away her child, forced the woman to make the choice between good and evil, as seen from the police point of view.

In addition, that back-stage discourses of moral judgments and ascriptions of the public's ignorance are not, unlike most other hidden transcripts, made public more often may be dysfunctional for society as a whole. Disseminating that discourse publicly would be an unpopular step with officers and with image-conscious police departments, and it would impede the work of cops; they would be less likely to get cooperation from subjects if they were seen as passing judgment of any kind—not that this does not leak out, either directly by speech or indirectly by tone or manner. Presenting an impassive or neutral persona is as deliberate an act as an aggressive, accusatory response. Both are in the cops' impression management tool kit.

On the other hand, media can be blamed for promoting views of street reality that undermine real cop work. There are two examples worthy of mentioning here. The first is the good faith of the criminal. One media portrayal of an aspect of crime that I heard referred to over and over again as being a particularly ludicrous and dangerous misrepresentation by fictional law enforcement programs and films is that crooks generally keep their word. A situation that officers cite is the farrago in which a bad guy has a hostage, perhaps a woman shopper whom he has grabbed and threatened with a gun. A police officer confronts him. The crook announces, "Put your gun down or I'll shoot her!" As one cop told me derisively, "Any police officer who gives up his gun to a criminal for any reason is too fucking stupid to be a cop." Another said, "People have this TV image or something that there's some sort of code of honor between the cops and the crooks, you know, we'll keep our word, they'll keep their word. *Never* give up your gun. He'll shoot the hostage, he'll shoot you. He doesn't care."

Cops also claim that, picking up from this good-faith fantasy, people will often ask to be trusted and will express indignation when the cops refuse, even though doing so would be dangerous and foolish. We were called to a domestic dispute in an apartment. The woman was crying and had obviously been punched in the jaw and slapped hard. The man was in his undershorts and bare feet, but he was extremely calm and polite. He stood on the second floor of the two-story apartment. The officer in charge remained at the bottom of the stairs and requested that the husband descend so that they could talk. The man asked to go back into his bedroom to get fully dressed first. The officer said, "No, you will come down right now." The man again insisted on putting on socks and shirt. The officer put his hand on his holster and ordered the man to immediately come downstairs. Man: *PP:* "I'm not violent, officer. I just wanna get dressed. What's the problem?" Cop: "The problem is I don't want you to come downstairs with a gun and kill me." The man protested, "I wouldn't do that. I'm not violent." The cop gave up on the dialogue, rushed up the stairs, and grabbed the guy. The backup officer followed instantly. Both of them pushed the man down onto the carpet and handcuffed him to be taken in for arrest. All the way to the station, he complained about his unfair treatment. Again, reality worlds collide. Perhaps the man had no intention of violence toward the officers; perhaps that was his legitimate self-perception. The cops could not be sure, and they had evidence from the wife otherwise; they did not want to take the risk.

When they give lectures to community groups, cops stress that one of the most important facts of crime prevention for people to absorb is that criminals lie about their intentions. In a TV situation, a criminal might grab a woman and say, "Let's go to your bank. I just want your money; I'm not gonna hurt you." As one cop declared, "It's pretty safe to assume that whatever a criminal tells you, you should believe the opposite, or the worst." It is an area of some controversy, but generally law enforcement personnel advise that you never let anyone take you away to another location that will most likely end up being the so-called "second crime scene." What the criminal wants, say the police, is to "get you away from the public place, to some ditch somewhere where they can rape and murder you."

Only a detailed content analysis of televisual portrayals of victim-criminal interaction might determine the verity of what cops say about what people see on TV. But again, the point is that the "stupidity" of the public about various aspects of law enforcement and crime is seen as directly related to mass media representations. What cops comment on in the back stage is a product of their perceptions of the dominant influence on the public's front-stage behavior.

A final dysfunctional type of public stupidity that can be an irritant to the officer and an impediment to law enforcement is the question of what constitutes a situation or a problem for which it is necessary to call in the police. The public is not trained in what exactly the police are able or sanctioned to do. In SLP, I saw the police summoned for just about every human predicament except a broken garbage disposal. Perhaps because the officers responded to medicals, we saw the most common exploitation in emergency services: people who called the police to get a ride to the hospital, not because they were desperately ill but because they wanted to avoid a taxicab charge. Their reasons may be understandable, but this is a case in which the cop is asked to do something outside of his prerogative. Barking dog complaints are another example; people are surprised to find that cops cannot confiscate a neighbor's vocal mutt. But the broadest area of nuisance call is the police officer asked to solve a personal dispute, that is, one that does not legitimately belong in the legal system, nor can the police officer "play the role" that the public expects.

Another living stereotype appears here: the out-of-control teenage son of the single mother. The litany is familiar. The kid has grown bigger than his mom has, he will not obey her, he hangs around with wild friends, and he is insulting, disobedient, and at times physically abusive. Rarely will the parent frame the situation as being that the kid himself is wild; rather, she will cite outside influences. Cops get the call even when Junior has not done anything specific. "Could you talk to him? Could you set him straight?" the mother will ask.

It is a tricky position for the officer. He is not a social worker; for the system-wise teen offender, there is actually little the officer can threaten. But sometimes an officer will agree to have a conversation with the son; at other times, he will contend that he cannot play that role. In these situations, I never got the sense or saw the evidence that one chat from a police officer could "make a difference." "They might turn around," said one officer, "but by the time they're shoving their mom and smoking pot all day there's not much we can do." Although cops do not believe that, to borrow a stereotype from psychology, it is all over by age 3, they assume that years of dysfunctionality will not be dissipated by a quick fix, whether it involves threats or fatherly counsel.[3]

This seems to be another instance in which the real cop cannot live up to the expectations of televisual reality. Again, I cannot speak for the public except to say that it is obvious that the mother wants a solution, immediately. She has realized that she is in the house with a 16-year-old "monster" (her term) and is increasingly exasperated, if not desperate. Whether this is the result of televisual acculturation about quick fixes and closures and psychological divine intervention, the product of the ancient human propensity toward self-delusion, or both is not the realm of this study to determine. But people are stupid, and this is one area of their stupidity. Cops, I interpret, believe that part of the basis of that stupidity is the absorption of the exaggerated powers of healing and helping, of solving and succoring, that TV cops, in their various guises, uniformly display. Indeed, the main duty of cops is often to counsel and divert juveniles rather than assist in their prosecution. Keeping records and tabs, the surveillance and bureaucratic functions of police work, are the typical responses to juvenile malfeasance (Meehan, 1993). The problem with this system, however, is that the targets of their warnings, the juveniles themselves, are sophisticated in their awareness of it. Hence, deterrence for future criminality is low, especially for the so-called minor first offences.

On the other hand, stupidity on the part of the public is a necessary prerequisite to successful policing, at least when those being stupid are suspects or perpetrators and their stupidity allows more efficacious police work. To paraphrase what a detective in the department said to me, if people really knew the law cold, the whole system would grind to a halt. He added, "Even worse than it is now." What people want from a police officer depends on the situation, but if they are the victims of a crime, they want the officer, within reason and sometimes beyond reason, to offer solutions, closure, and reparations. The legal system may provide such amends but only after a much longer time and a much more tortuous effort than anyone outside of readers of *Bleak House* have an idea of. A cop confided to me once, after arresting someone on an assault charge, *PP:* "In a way, the victim's nightmare is just beginning. At least this guy [the perp] knows what he's up against. The victim has no idea." In this fashion, it is actually helpful that people are not completely aware of their full rights and responsibilities when facing the law. Television may provide some list of these—the notorious technicalities produced by liberal judges and unctuous defense lawyers—but on the street, legalism is synonymous with gridlock.

A common example is the cops' arrival at a residence doorway. On television, doors pose very little challenge to police officers. A knock, someone is home, perhaps the door is opened a crack, may we come in, flash badge; or in moments of greater action, a knock, a noise, and the door is kicked in. I never saw, in 2 years at SLP-PD, a door kicked in; the irony is that, at least under Minnesota law, the flimsiest particleboard door is a stout barrier to the police officer. In fact, an officer cannot enter a house unless an occupant invites him in, or if he suspects that criminal activity is occurring behind the door, or if he believes that someone's health or life is in jeopardy. The first situation is the most likely avenue for gaining entrance to a house. The best way to keep a cop out of your house is not to answer the door; technically, only a search warrant would allow entry. These conditions of course produce their own humor. Standing outside a doorway attempting to arrest someone on a warrant, a cop senses that someone is inside but is not answering the door; another officer pipes in a Mickey Mouse voice, "Come in!" Or mimicking the late-night TV commercial, "I've fallen, and I can't get up!" This became a common enough joke when I rode along that I provided my own variation, drawn, of course, from television. With a bass profundo, I would bellow, "Help me, Spock! Help me!"

I never witnessed an officer use this gambit in earnest. It is another case of the cops' sensibility being checkmated by their commonsense. Hunches are part of the equation, but legalism and technicalities interfere with the playing of them. A cop might whisper to me in the hallway: "He's behind the door, I know it. He's laughing at us." But if there is no answer, eventually we must walk away. The anticlimax is noted dutifully: "You could have gotten a picture of me busting it down—just like on TV." He adds, *PP:* "And then you would have gotten a picture of me being chewed out by the captain."

Yet, what saves the police officer from endlessly encountering frustration is the fact that most people are unaware of their rights, and cops are not required, under the law, to volunteer them. You knock on a door; a guy who is wanted on three warrants for assault and rape opens it. *PP:* "Are you Mr. Smith?" "Yeah." "We'd like to come in and talk to you." "Okay." The cops then march in and cuff him. In other cases, physical intimidation plays a role. Registered in the eyes of the person at the door is the impression—or at least I thought I saw it there— that they are afraid the cops will break the door down unless it is opened for them. Once, an interchange occurred on this subject. While cuffing a man—a noise complaint turned into an arrest for domestic assault—who had "opened up," the cop said, *PP:* "Buddy, why did you let us in? You could have just shut up and not answered the door." The man responded, "I thought I had to let cops in." After booking the suspect, the cop at one point told me, "Thank God they [the public] watch too many *Cops* shows—they [TV cops] never walk away from a door."

Another hazier area of legalism versus pragmatism involves the dreaded "L-word": lawyer. When a cop arrests someone, he really does read the Miranda rights, including "You have the right to consult legal counsel." Cops are amazed at how rarely people avail themselves of this right, especially the incredibly guilty, the criminal who knows this is a serious inquiry and who is facing lengthy jail time. The goal of a police officer to some extent and the detective completely is to get as much information out of the suspect as possible before he or she utters the fatal sentence: "I wanna speak to my lawyer." A detective recounted a questioning session to the lunch crowd at the squad room. "We were pretty close [to a confession] and then boom! The L-word. And it all shut down." The entrance of a lawyer indicates that the legal system, that clunky, irrational, gasping, glacially paced machine, has now entered the game.

Limited knowledge of the law on the part of the public also assists officers in the case of juveniles. Ironically, the "bad" teens—chronically delinquent, always in and out of trouble with the cops, and indeed recognizable by face and on a first-name basis with every officer in the department—knew best that the system was "a joke." They understood that the worst punishment meted out for vandalizing a car would be a letter of reprimand. A court date offered no terror for them. In contradistinction, the "good" kids, those who had only a single brush with the law, were the least knowledgeable of their rights and responsibilities and most terrified at the prospect of court or juvenile hall. Cops would often recite to wayward teenagers the maximum penalties for criminal behavior ("what is gonna happen to you if you don't fly straight"), which, realistically in the Minnesota system, would rarely be administered. Again, I think it is the consensus of police officers that if everyone had an intimate knowledge of the law code that the system itself would collapse, and the courts would grind to a halt as opposed to a slow crawl.

Relatedly, parents who "don't know what their kids are up to" are both considered stupid and are targets for moral castigation. The clueless parent is a common stereotype held by police officers. It is also one that, as in so many other cop stereotypes, seems genuinely confirmed by their daily experience. *PP:* "Dad's not home, mom's not home, they're at work, they're divorced, whatever. It doesn't matter if the kids are rich or poor, the parents don't know what they're doing." Another cop offered, "We know kids better than their parents do." A further insight: "Parents don't wanna know. They don't want to hear it." This is as close as cops come to being sociologists, but it is always tinged with the more traditionalist notion of society's moral failure and lack of personal responsibility. Its counterpoint is that cops do know, cops are "there" and have access to the true character of the delinquent teenager.

A host of encounters in which parents are confronted with the bad behavior of their children could be cited, one of which I found particularly poignant and literally close to home. Across the street from the apartment building in which

I lived was a single-family dwelling. I had never met anyone who resided there but had seen once or twice an Asian woman mowing the lawn. One day while patrolling we got a call to the house. The woman complained that her daughter had been threatened at school by some other kids, and then, the mother alleged, those same kids had come by the house and thrown rocks, cracking one of the windows. Racial epithets were yelled as well. The daughter was a poster child of model minority innocuousness: slight, thick glasses, bookish. We readily believed she could be a victim at the local junior high school. The leader of the pack of taunters and rock throwers was identified. She lived only a couple of blocks away in an apartment complex. We drove over. The accused daughter was not home from school, but her mother was there. The officer described the rock-throwing incident and the accusation. The woman offered a blanket denial: *PP:* "That's not my daughter. I didn't raise her to do such things. It must have been somebody else. She has some friends I disapprove of; maybe she just happened to be standing by."

This time there was a "movie moment." The daughter then walked in. We had not asked the mother whether her daughter had ever been in trouble with the police. The woman talked to her daughter in front of us, obviously seeking assurance that the girl was not responsible for the episode. The 14-year-old unleashed a torrent of expletives and abuse. She admitted that not only had she been there, but she also led the incident. She cursed the Asian girl, cursed her mother, the police, the world. The mother fulfilled her stereotype as well. *PP:* "Where did you learn such language?" The girl was almost laughing at her mother now: "This is the language I always fucking use. This is my fucking language. Where've you been?" The cop interjected. There was only so much we could do. The girl was underage; the incident was minor. She knew, and we knew, that at most she would get a warning or a letter of reprimand. No one was satisfied with the closure of the incident, least of all the cop or myself.

Moral judgment, which I joined in, was swift, however. The cop began, "Boy, that mom just had no idea—clueless." I asked him, "Do you think it was an act for our benefit?" He answered, "No, parents really are that stupid. They just build this wrong image of their kids. We see the kids in a completely other light, and the parents just don't get it. She got it today, though." I asked if he thought that the mother here had learned what her daughter was really like. He shook his head: *PP:* "They'll argue, and then that little future biker chick there will be sweet and kind to her mother for 5 minutes and her mother will instantly forgive her. Parents like that never change. They want to be clueless." The discussion shifted to the reasons for the daughter's character. "Divorced, dad not in the picture, bitter mother, asshole boyfriends; take your pick."

Police officers have a plethora of suppositions to explain the public's conduct, and it would be tempting for an outside observer, especially one familiar with social-scientific reasoning, to conclude that cops attribute overly simplistic reasons for behavior. This is not the case. Cops understand poverty, broken homes, child abuse, and neglect. Most cops themselves are from poorer or working-class backgrounds. The same cannot necessarily be said about most sociologists and criminologists. But although general explanations can be offered for crime and for criminal behavior, cops deal with individuals, not aggregates; flesh-and-blood human beings, not hypotheses and generalizations based on statistical models. If a defiant kid refuses to take his hand out of his pocket (where he may be holding a weapon), sociology can be of no help to him or the cop who confronts him. Likewise, for a cop dealing with his exasperation at a reckless, criminally prone, surly, abusive teenager, mom, dad, and the kid herself or himself are the only opportune targets for moral disapproval; there is simply no satisfaction in blaming society. Again, to ascribe such feelings to ego validation is not to undermine objective reality as perceived by the police officer. As is clear from my own voice here, after 2 years of confronting such kids and witnessing such parents, I found it almost impossible to accept any theory of human action that did not place a premium on personal responsibility for oneself and for one's children. The street cannot teach any other lesson.

The most categorical moral sanction officers placed on people was, "We'll see him again" or "we'll be back." It was the coda to encounters in which cops felt that they had interacted with a member of the criminal class, a born or nurtured "bad guy."[4] An incident in which I participated to a greater extent than I was willing illustrates the mechanics of how, in some cases, cops actually receive the feedback that validates their moral judgments. These are my notes (edited to conceal identities) taken after the fact; reciting the incident in full captures the flavor of the moment and my reaction:

Call at X apts. A woman and her husband—both huge—are chasing an [older] man. She accuses him of molesting her. She keeps screaming, "He saw me in shorts and he says he wants to have sex with me." He is about half her size and looks terrified, less of us than of her. He denies this. She is drunk. Her husband is drunk, or stoned. Alcohol is strong on her, at least; both have slurred speech. The chased man steps aside with Officer Tom. Officer Hugo takes charge of the woman. Officer Len and I face the husband. He starts telling us how there shouldn't be any jails, that people should just be shamed. We say nothing, but he keeps getting closer to me. Finally, he looks at me and says, "You look like a fag, man." He proposes to fight and insists that's what shows he's a man. I'm frozen—it's fight or flight.[5] Len smiles, letting things happen. I may actually have to fight; I think about taking off my glasses first but I'm blind without them. Then the husband runs away: no reason, certainly not from my intimidation. They don't chase him. They walk back with the woman. She keeps yelling loud, louder. Tom asks her to go in. He asks her why her husband ran. She says because they were "oppressing" him. Hugo gets angry and says that a real man would not run away from where his wife is with cops at 2 a.m. She doesn't want to go inside. Hugo gives her a minute or the detox. She announces that she will have her private parts tested to see whose sperm is in them.

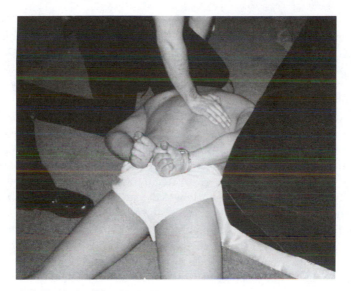

Figure 5.2.

But she goes inside. In the squad car, Tom nods to me: *"We'll be back at their place soon."*

And, lo! The prophecy was fulfilled:

Domestic in progress—back. It is the woman in the parking lot. Her brother is outside saying the husband is acting like a "wild man." Cops go in. Daughter and son are with crying wife. Now she begs for help; her face is bruised. Door to bedroom is locked. They try to pry it open with badge pin. He won't open door. They kick it open. Wrestle him into cuffs [See Figure 5.2]. He claims he doesn't know what they are doing it for. But at the station he calls them fags.

My own gratification was kept in the back stage, of course. I took no pleasure in the woman's pain, but as rider in the squad car and wearer of the uniform, I felt no small satisfaction in my moral judgment being confirmed.

Rationalizing Back-Stage Transcripts

It would seem from such examples that the back stage is a place of shady business and rampant denigration of everyone else. It is clear, however, that the back stage itself serves a vital purpose for the cohesiveness of any group, not exclusively street police officers. No human being is as frustrated as one who has no place to complain, to talk rough, to screw around, to crack jokes, to trade insults, to make self-validating observations—that is, to be human. I will add my own feeling here—because at times I greatly sympathized with the plight of the officers in situations of tension, frustration, exasperation, exhaustion, and suppressed anger, I felt a sense of release to be able to climb back in the squad car and talk about what had just happened or even just shake my head and say, "Can you believe that guy?" Retroactive discursive vindication was better than none at all. The back stage, thus, was an antidote to much of what the cops faced on the front stage or, to use another analogy, a decompression chamber from the high-pressure moments on the street. Although police departments and publics have the right to sometimes uncover nefarious doings of the back stage, the existence of a back stage itself and the maintenance of some level of security of its transcripts are important to the survival of the street officer and, inevitably, her or his mission to serve and protect the citizenry.

In addition, it is unclear whether a full revelation of the back stage at all times, to everyone, would serve any purpose or would gratify any true public yearning. It is often said that the best evidence that powers of telepathy are not widespread is that more people are not killing each other for what they think about each other. The necessary lies of politeness and propriety are part of all human interchanges, whether at academic conferences, advertising agency meetings, or police car stops. The public, I suspect, has some prurient interest in the police back stage. It is part of the popularity of cop shows that we see their goings-on in the squad room or at a bar after work, or even in bed with a lover. But it is a question that only other ethnographies and survey research might answer: Whether people facing problems on the street and in their homes would simply prefer the cop to play his agreed-on front-stage role and have little interest and perhaps some fear in learning anything of the back stage. When, as in a case I witnessed, a young woman is in tears because she lost her engagement ring in a restaurant, I am not sure she really wants to hear or if it would serve any purpose in telling her that if the ring is not turned in right away, she will never see it again. What she wants to hear is, "We'll enter it into the files. If it's sold anywhere legally, we'll know about it. It's possible you'll get it back. These things have turned up. We'll work on it." However important the back stage might be for the cop, what people really want is that the cop play well his front-stage role and, like an actor, at least for the length of the performance, convince them of its authenticity and sincerity.

Is this characterization of the public unfair? One officer's claim that "all we do is adult day care" seems unduly sweeping. Anecdotes are not aggregates. Cops, as said, meet "bad" people or "good" people in moments of distress. Nobody calls a cop to witness or intervene in a pleasant situation. But anecdotes encrust on each other and form the bedrock for experience and for beliefs. Stories such as those told here can serve as yet another confirmation of the fickleness, arrogance, and plain stupidity of the public. That the same "stupid" people may in their other lives be sharp stockbrokers, eloquent teachers, dazzlingly competent chefs, dexterous and diligent mechanics, or anything else does not mean that in the cop's realm they do not get addled. Police, then, are aware that their value judgments are unfair to many good people but do describe people in the persona that they meet every day, on call, on the street.

STAR POWER AND CONTROL

Not all stage players are created equal: Hierarchy exists in any ritual, public or private. To say that the police officer is the star of the drama is a metaphorical exaggeration, but it does explain the tension inherent in his role in modern society. Primed by expectations from the TV world, people think (so cops believe) that cops should solve problems, bring closure, and enact justice. At the same time, almost in contradiction, negative stereotypes—the swollen-bellied donut chomper, the corrupt thug, the blockhead—play into the mix of how the public perceives the cop. But from the cop's point of view, it is his or her right and duty to be star of the dramas in which he or she appears. This duty, however, is as frustrated by the conventions of law and the realities of the street as is any impulse of a human actor. To some extent, cops feel that the system, the public, or reality itself does not allow them to fully exploit their role. Establishing some degree of authority in officer-citizen encounters is both the police officer's main concern and his main difficulty. Without this authority, the police officer cannot control the situation. These encounters are usually brief and between strangers with little knowledge of each other, situations in which police are usually at a numerical disadvantage; establishing control is, therefore, essential.

Star power is thus exerted and measured by control over a situation and people. Figure 5.3 shows a perhaps overly obvious illustration of the control a police officer may have in a situation—in this case, a stereotypical situation. The call had the usual minimal data to process. *PP:* "Teenagers seen trying to break into the local school after hours. The person who reported it thinks he may have seen a gun." We arrived just as three teenagers emerged running from behind the school building. They froze at the sight of cops jumping out of their cruisers. The policemen ordered the boys to pull their hands out of their pockets. The boys did not obey. Guns were drawn.

PP: "Down, down. Get on the ground and spread out, face down. Keep your hands where I can see them." This time, the teenagers acquiesced. The racial implications of the moment were apparent in the picture but less so at the scene. I believed the officers would have given the same commands and reacted the same way to white teenagers. The boys remained prone, and the officers searched them, finding nothing. A brief dialogue ensued. The officers became convinced that these kids had nothing to do with the call. They were released. We never did find anyone else around. The encounter was classified as Gone on Arrival; there was no closure or resolution.

This two-step process of enacting control was common, especially in the interaction with teenage boys. There always seems to be an initial show of resistance: This was especially true when in the presence of peers.[6] An officer

Figure 5.3.

told me, "I guess nobody likes to back down instantly. It's worse of course if they've got their girlfriends around." The teenagers are defying the power of the cop; they are refusing to place themselves immediately under his control. The officer escalates the situation with a verbal threat. At this point, almost all suspects back down. What is clear, though, is that to some extent, this is a ritualistic interaction, almost like an audience calling out to a performer to engage in a characteristic line or stage trick. "It's a game," another cop said. "They play with our heads. We play with their heads." It is a game that the cop almost always wins, but it is interesting to speculate that the other players in the game might have their own moment of satisfaction: *PP:* "You really told that cop off," or "Man, did you see that cop's face?" One need not dig too deeply into the teenage boy's zeitgeist to consider that provoking an adult is in itself a satisfying activity, especially in light of the self-perception of immunity from real legal sanctions and the indestructibility of teenage existence. So in one sense, the cop's reputation for using physical force is a legitimate extension of his work practices. It would be difficult to find another way of policing that would not result in teenagers pushing the limits even further or end with more cops killed by people who really did have guns in their pockets.

Another incident, which occurred during one of my first patrols with the SLP officers, typified the issues of dominance and submission that define control of the "street" and, by proxy, the cop's status (see Figure 5.4). The episode

Figure 5.4.

began with a call that a teenager was either threatening or showing a gun to people in the local McDonald's. When we arrived, there were, as is often the case, a host of suspects, many young men who answered the description of a "white teenager wearing baseball cap." As is also typical, many would not show their hands or empty their pockets: glares, sneers, and surliness were the response to the officer's request. To any other adult, this is teen normalcy. To the police, it is a signal of danger and an ego-invalidating challenge to their authority. Teenagers must never be allowed to humiliate a cop in public, so to reestablish their authority and alleviate the danger, the police treat everyone the same: line up to be searched. The young men complain; no doubt they feel aggrieved. They know they are innocent; they do not understand why they are being picked on. Neither side is willing to understand the origin of the others' fears, cautions, and behavior: Neither has the time or the inclination.

The scene shown in Figure 5.5 followed moments later when a woman drove up, informing us that two kids were seen running down a nearby street, one with gun in hand. We jumped in the squad car and raced to the area. There were only two young men in sight. The officers got out of the squad and ordered the youths to "spread 'em" on the car. The boys hesitated; one refused and cursed the officer. Finally the officers drew guns and started screaming at the teens to turn around and assume "the position." This they finally did. They were searched, and no gun was found, but after a long shouting match, one of the boys led the cops to the gun, which they had tossed into the bushes. It was in fact a toy gun, though it was painted black to look real. The cops had concluded

Figure 5.5.

the incident by raising the stakes to the maximum short of actual gunplay; that this is what it took to gain control, to enact compliance from the teenagers, is a comment on to what extent cops feel their status is under continual challenge.

The gamesmanship of power is thus common. If cops play their game, so do citizens, innocent bystanders, crooks, and surly teenagers. In any such game, the results need not be zero sum. A teenage boy's sense of rebellion and self-righteousness can be nourished as much as a cop's feeling of "getting the job done." This was put forth in a discussion by a couple of cops one night in the squad room. "You can have fun pushing people's buttons. It's pathetic, sometimes." Another cop said, "Sometimes the most crazy types, I mean the lethal weapons, will go to jail like a baby if you treat them with respect." The first cop added, "And if you don't, it's easy to toss a hand grenade at some of these guys." In short, the last realm of power of the police officer before the gun is actually fired or a punch is thrown is verbal manipulation. They are aware that they themselves can, by their language or even their tone, create an incident or douse one; so, of course, can the public they encounter. Negotiating the cop's status, as well as defining its boundaries, is a social issue, one that should be at the front stage of public debate about what role police should play.

From these circumstances arise one of the most significant issues relating the street to the mediated police: the arrogance of teens. It requires no great cultural insight or content analysis to say that we live in the era of the superteen: The teenager is courted as the preferred demographic of material and media products. TV and movie teens are complex: They range from the clueless of the movie of the same name to the wise rebels of *Titanic*. In discussions about mediated teens, however, cops remarked on how different the street version they encountered was. *PP:* "True, we tend to meet the ones who make mistakes, or who do bad things, but damned if they will admit that." The surly teen, supremely confident in his hipness and sense of entitlement, scornful of law and adults, was a constant irritant: "They think they know everything." To exacerbate matters, "On TV, teenagers are always right; adults are goofs." On the street, the distinction is less fine: Both adults and teens can be "stupid." The frustration is that the teen is perceived as having even less right to disrespect the cop. One officer tells a young man, "You think you're so smart now. Well, are you smarter than you were 7 years ago?" The reply is a grudging, "Yeah." The rejoinder, "Well, what makes you think that you won't be smarter 7 years from now?" The breakdown in adult authority—for which cops blame media and parents—thus makes their work significantly less pleasant and returns less in the coin of respect that cops feel they deserve.

FAILED EXPECTATIONS AND VALUE JUDGMENTS

The role of cops as star is undermined by the fact that people want attention to be paid to them. But, as said, one of the myths of police work is that of focus. The frame of the film or television screen is obviously limited, and except in rare cases, only one time and place are depicted in a given scene. This endows a sense of significance to the narrative—that the events are of consequence within the scheme of society, that the cop is tending to the problem at hand. But cops know that other calls may be waiting and that these might be more important. For example, an officer tries to deal quickly with a barking dog complaint because an assault call is pending, and the department is overtaxed. In addition, people's narratives or descriptions tend to include information that to police is both redundant and extraneous. In contrast, televisual narratives are edited and to the point, whether they are defined as factual news or fictional drama. Finally, although people may think that a detailed explanation of their situation will result in a bypassing of standard procedures, the police officer assisting them may respond that he or she cannot do what is asked because it is contrary to administration regulations.

This demand for exceptionalism and the disregard for legalism can range from the minor to the major. For example, it was a recently implemented policy of the department to no longer assist motorists who had locked their keys in the car. There are several practical reasons cited for not providing what used to be an assumed public service of cops. First and foremost was the ever-present consideration of the lawsuit. Too many people, the administration stated and the city lawyers cautioned, could sue the police department, claiming that their car had been damaged when officers tried to get the door open. A second reason of lesser importance was that in modern automobiles, it is actually much more difficult to pop open a door, so cops might fail to do it. This would mean a loss of face (i.e., "We can't do something we told you we could do."). This rule is sometimes overlooked: If a little old lady was stuck by the road late at night after accidentally locking her keys inside, a cop would gladly bend policy to help her out.

The stated exception to this policy was for a threat to life or potential for injury: for example, a child trapped in a hot car. Gradually, it filtered to the public that the police would no longer open their locked cars for them, save in this case. This led to potential confrontation because, as we know, people lie. There was a call. A woman had locked her keys in a car in a parking lot. The officer checked with the dispatcher: "Anybody inside?" The dispatcher called the officer on his cellular phone (thus not recorded on police channels) to say that the caller at first reported only that her keys were locked in. Then, when the dispatcher explained that they could only help out if someone was in danger, the woman added, "Oh, yeah, my baby is in the car."

The officer shrugged. *PP:* "What the heck." We arrived in the parking lot. I made an instant leap of class stereotype that was expressed verbally by the officer: "Wouldn't you know: a Mercedes." A Mercedes, as I learned, was shorthand for prejudice that the driver was a rich snob. A worried executive-looking woman stood by the driver's door and waved us down. The officer winked at me and jumped out of his squad car. "How can I help?" His tone bordered on mocking. The woman told us about the keys locked in the car. "But where's the baby?" he asked. She said, "Well, there must have been a misunderstanding." He replied, "We were told that there was a baby in the car, a baby in danger. What happened to the baby?" The woman squirmed on the axis of her high heels and then blurted out, "Well, I had to get you to come. I have to get to an appointment." The officer explained that he really could not help her, that he was not very good at this sort of thing, and that a Mercedes is really tough to open. Would she consider calling the auto club? He noticed the AAA sticker on her bumper. "But they take at least half an hour!" she protested.

I could swear that instead of any feeling of being in the wrong, of lying to the police, of technically filing a false report, of treating a police officer like a private servant, the woman looked aggrieved. The cop and I discussed the incident while driving away. The officer laughed, "Tonight at dinner she'll tell her husband about how a cop wouldn't help her when she was in trouble." People's minor inconveniences must be paid attention to; that is the impression I got from looking over the shoulders of the police and through their windshields.

But the demand for making things right extends much further. An incident, as summed up in my notes:

> Show up at a small brown house. We got a call about a violation of an order of protection. Guy seen driving near house of teenage girl. Her mother is there. She is divorced from dad and has an order of protection against him. The cops do not find him or see him. The officer explains that he can't issue a warrant based upon a sighting by a citizen. The woman is irate—why can't he?

The cop tried to explain. He was unable to simply take her word; it's the law. It is another example of people wanting justice, not law, of wanting exceptions to fit in their self-appraisal of being good citizens. In our postincident processing, the cop said, "They just can't believe I won't break the law for them." He understood their plight and even sympathized with them; the ex-husband was probably a "bad guy."

The greatest tension occurs when cops, contrary to sympathizing with the plea for justice or attention in a citizen they encounter, feel that it is undeserving or fraudulent. An example: a car accident. It looked like just a fender bender. One driver, however, was splayed out in his seat, head back, breathing shallowly. He said, *PP:* "I hit my head. I can hardly see. I can hardly breathe." The cops were first on the scene. They put an oxygen mask on him, waiting for the paramedics. The officer I was riding with gave me "the look." It was the glance of extreme dubiousness, the "there's something rotten here" expression. The paramedics arrived; the police let them take over. Walking back to the squad car the officer said, "That guy was faking it." *PP:* "He doesn't have a bruise on him. It wasn't more than a 10 mile per hour collision." He added, "He'll probably get away with it, too." The cop's disgust level climaxed when he felt that someone was trying to trick him and that the system, which in many ways he has little faith in, would perpetuate the fraud. What could he do? There was a report to write, in which he would, in as clear terms as possible, point out the condition of the car, the probable speed of impact, and the lack of bruising on the man's face. He hoped that an insurance investigator would note such details. If asked by the company, he could even pass on the inference from those facts as well. Perhaps, by such a method, he could dispense his justice circuitously.

It is remarkable sometimes how the spiral of cynicism that cops might justifiably fall into about their own abilities to fulfill the public's wishes can be arrested and other feelings and emotions produced instead. Hence, we cannot generalize and say that when people ask cops to do something that they really are not supposed to do, they always react with irritation and exasperation. Pathos, for example, and empathy or sympathy were often evident. In one call, one of the more sober and cynical cops sat down with a young woman who reported an assault to the dispatcher. A few minutes into the discussion, however, she said that she just did that to get a cop to come help her. She was a pregnant teenager; her father was out of the picture, and her mother was at work. She did not know what to do. The obvious question: "What's your relationship with the father of the child?" The depressingly familiar answer, *PP:* "It's one of two guys." She seemed somewhat unsure that the field was narrowed to only these two. Here the incident could have entered the legal domain. Both men were in their 20s; she was 15. Did she know their names? She said, *PP:* "No, one I met at a party, and his name's Jim something. The other was Jim something's friend." She thought they were from Chicago. Did that help?

The course of the conversation took a surprising turn. I expected the cop to pursue the possible legal ramifications of statutory rape. But instead, he started counseling the girl. He gave her the numbers of some social workers, suggested that she have a conversation with her mother, and then consider her options. It was about 15 minutes of talk, which is quite a long interaction between public and cop without any mention of crime or criminality. He was being a little bit of a father and a little more of a social worker. When we finally left, the girl was smiling. She promised to talk to her mother. Whether she did or not and what the resolution might have been is something we do not know. In the squad car, the cop said, "They're so dumb at that age, but she could be my daughter." He could not, with a wave of his wand or a flash of his badge, make things better, but he could take 20 minutes of his day to listen, calmly and consolingly. Sometimes this is all people want from a cop—not a concrete solution, but sober counsel. Or, more often, they want an authority figure in navy blue to officially pronounce for them that their problem is legitimate, that "that's tough" or "that's terrible; yes, you have been victimized. You are a victim."

In many cases, people also express moralistic judgments about themselves and ask for the cops' approval. The verbal cues for requesting such sanctions typically involve a repetitive assertion of one's own moral worth or absolution in comparison to the perfidy or malfeasance of others. A couple arrived at the station to bail out their son who had been driving with a suspended license. Talking to the desk sergeant while the papers were being filed and processed, the couple stated a total of 14 times in 5 minutes that "we're good parents" or some version of "we didn't bring him up this way." The sergeant did what might come naturally to a human being in such circumstances: He nodded in agreement and occasionally said, "Well, you don't know with kids. We get a lot of good parents in here" (I don't think he meant this facetiously).

In another case, a woman was apprehended for shoplifting by the security guard at a local mall. She put some cheap earrings in her pocket and walked out the door but had been recorded by the department store security camera. She was a stereotype of an inoffensive homemaker; no one would have labeled her as a criminal. When I arrived with the cop, she also stated within a 10-minute span, 21 times according to my tick book, a variation of "I'm a good person." The cop did not attend to the greater number of these pleas while taking the information report from the store, whose responsibility it was to provide enough evidence to press criminal charges; they had an "Always Charge" policy, no matter what the circumstance or the price of the item stolen. When the cop did face the woman, she continued with her protests. He did not comment on them but stated clearly that that was the way the law worked; it was not up to him. He did say that it was unlikely that any court would give her a harsh sentence or more than a warning. In the previous case, then, the desk sergeant enabled to some extent the moral judgment of the individuals. In the latter case, the cop offered no absolution.

Figure 5.6.

Often as well, people want cops to concur with their own negative moral judgments against others. A man's mailbox had been knocked down three times in the past month. The cop took the report, but the man was so irate he could barely provide his name or the dates of the other incidents. He was much more interested in having the cop agree with him. "I can't believe these kids nowadays. This isn't a prank; these are monsters." Or, "Parents today, they just don't know how to raise kids!" The cop did not disagree. While filling out the incident report, he nodded and occasionally chimed in during the man's diatribe against modern youth: "Yeah, we see that all the time. You should see some of the other stuff these kids do." Generally, a police officer is quite willing to agree with indictments of the teenage species.

But in other circumstances, an officer will not only refuse to concur with a moral judgment but will explicitly state that one is uncalled for or irrelevant, the "pox on both your houses" verdict (see Figure 5.6). Two sisters were engaging in a blistering early morning argument outside an apartment building. Neighbors had complained about the noise. The women were so caught up in their fury that they hardly noticed the cops arriving. The lead cop tried to restore order, but the women persisted in their dispute. Finally, he shut them down, threatening to take both of them into custody for disturbing the peace. He took one woman over to one side; his backup took the sister into her apartment. I stayed with the lead cop. The woman offered, in a profusion of expletives, a long series of crimes and misdemeanors that her sister had committed against her: stealing her boyfriend, taking money, backstabbing her, breaking her things, and so on. The cop listened to this, then told her, "Okay, I want you to stay right here, and I don't want you to move." He went to confer with the other officer, separate from the two women. I joined them. The other sister apparently had given much the same story, with the first sister cast as villainess.

It is clear as well that neither of them wanted to file charges; they just wanted somebody to declare a victory. The declamation I overheard was peppered with implications and assertions of "I'm good," "I'm right," and "she's bad." The cop would have none of this. He called them both together, suggested that one move to another part of the city and that being roommates was not such a good idea, and said that if he had to come back someone would go to jail, probably both of them. Both women were left chastened but still registered expressions of mute protest and moral aggrievement. As we left, the lead cop shrugged—what can you do? And he commented, "We'll be back." We were, an hour later, for another noise complaint against the pair. Whether or not the women were looking for a referee, it was clear that they wanted someone to lay down who was morally right. However, their demand for justice could not be fulfilled by anyone, not even a cop.

It would be unreasonable to say that cops always have distancing or negative reactions to the demands for justice. They are equally rewarded by them; after all, to some extent, they justify their job as doing good, and only part of that doing good is the enforcement of law. If their own knowledge and acumen are relatively enhanced by encountering the stupid deceitful, then their feeling of doing good is enhanced by assisting those who obviously cannot help themselves. Sometimes, in these cases, the concordance with a mass media image is commented on. There was a call that a very young boy had been seen walking up and down a street for almost an hour. We arrived. He was a tow-headed lad, the body double of Opie from the *Andy Griffith Show,* complete with chipped tooth and slight lisp. He seemed to be about 7 or 8; he was still at the stage of saying, "Yes, Mr. Policeman" and "No, Mr. Policeman." His story was confused, but apparently he was dropped off by the baby-sitter, and his mother was not home as he had expected. It was 2 o'clock on a weekday, and there were no neighbors around. Even the person who had made the call was not home or would not answer the door.

We decided to camp out on the step for a little while. The officer talked about good old-fashioned little boy stuff—fishing, soccer—and shared a stick of gum with Opie. The boy asked to go for a ride in the police car. The officer obliged, taking him around the block, while I waited on the steps in case the mother showed up. They came back, we waited a little longer, and in a screech the mom did pull up, offering flustered apologies of miscuing with the baby-sitter and being stuck in traffic. She seemed sincere; no moral judgments were called for. The child was delivered to her safely. Good-byes were waved. The cop joked with me, "If I had a fatter ass and there was an ice cream parlor nearby, we could have restaged that Norman Rockwell painting [of a cop and a kid at a soda fountain] for you, Dave." It was a pleasant interlude. The cop didn't start whistling a tune, but obviously he had enjoyed helping out, and the happy ending was appropriate. He did not have to tell me that it made him feel good to be a cop in a situation like that, to be the only one around who shows up and helps in the atomistic suburb.

His actions and their resulting satisfaction also underline that the cop takes his power relationships as he finds them. We accord police the front stage, and we give them a legal sanction to express a degree of star power that few other actors on the public stage merit. The range of situations, in which such power is used, is vast, from shooting a fleeing killer to taking someone's child on a little ride around the block in the police car. If the front stage is where the action takes place and the back stage is where judgments on those actions and on the people encountered in the front stage are rendered, then we see the symbiotic relationship of the two orientations.

NOTES

1. One officer described why he never wore his uniform home: "Too many people hate cops. Just driving home, someone sees me in my pickup in cop uniform. Who knows what shit is out there?"

2. Indeed, some research has shown a high correlation between the "job satisfaction" of a police officer and the number of "best friends" they report having in the department (Slovak, 1978).

3. This prejudice is well supported by research on juvenile criminal behavior. Many studies, from a variety of methods, have found that high rates of misbehavior early in childhood are correlated with misbehavior (including criminal activity) in later life (Caspi, Bem, & Elder, 1989; Sampson & Laub, 1993). Cops' moral judgments, among which are that lax parenting may be one cause of that behavior, are also supported by research: Extremes of overdiscipline, erratic discipline, or laxity in parental control are good predictors of child misbehaver (Riley & Shaw, 1985; see also Sampson & Laub, 1993). In general, family socialization variables such as level of involvement with children and supervision are strong and clear predictors of delinquency (Loeber & Stouthamer-Loeber, 1986).

4. In one study by the Kansas City (Missouri) police, it was found that in 50% of domestic murders, the police had been called to intervene in a quarrel between the couple five or more times previously (Police Foundation, 1977). The irony in the designation of a "we'll see him again" sentiment is that cops, to use Ericson's (1982) phrase, seek to "reproduce order"; to have disorder spring up again in one's wake is, in a sense, a failure. At the same time, it is a minor triumph of psychological acuity to predict who will be, as one SLP cop put it, "the repeat customers."

5. I could feel the "fight-or-flee" response in myself: increased heart rate, tunnel vision, and faster breathing (see Selye, 1956).

6. Unsurprisingly, research on juvenile criminal activity suggests that delinquents tend to have other delinquents as their proximity peers, those they hang out with (Hindelang, Hirschi, & Weis, 1981). Furthermore, those peers are very likely to be the partners in delinquent activity (Erickson & Jenson, 1977).

The (Real) Mean World

As stated earlier, cops are "there" when "shit happens"; this produces a squad car windshield view of the world. There is no better way to define this perspective than with the term Gerbner and his associates used to describe the view of the heavy watcher of television: a *mean world,* a world where bad things are happening and danger lurks. Although it is true that the mean world of television rarely corresponds with the world as defined by crime statistics, cop encounters with the public are largely restricted to trauma, crime, medicals, tragedy, disaster, or at the least minor problems—never pleasant episodes. For most people, however, those events are deviance. Almost everyone will be in a car accident at least once or robbed, but even in the most crime-prone neighborhoods or accident-prone intersections, these are not daily occurrences for the individual civilian. For the cop, however, these are unsurprising, if not televisually paced, events of his work. Some—perhaps most—of a shift may be spent in undramatic activity; forms must be filed, endless driving done, lunch eaten, and conversation held with other cops. These too are realities of police work. But when something "happens," it is almost invariably bad, as defined by society. Sometimes the cop can prevent and protect, but usually he arrives after the evil that men and women do has already been committed. This undoubtedly contributes to the cops' cynical view of human nature, but it also generally contributes to an impression that the world itself is mean and full of danger (cf. Lester, 1979, 1987).

IN THE SAME BOAT

Cops have considerable reason to view themselves as separate from the rest of society. Part of the basis for this opinion is the almost unique position of police work, the cops' uniform, and their mandate in society. But the distinction comes as well from the physical-spatial relationship of cops to the outside world. Figure 6.1 displays the inside of one of the older models of a St. Louis

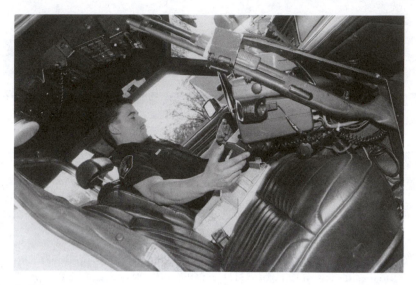

Figure 6.1.

Park (SLP) squad car. Most prominent is the bench seat, uncomfortable at the best of times, poorly designed for posture support; it is not an agreeable post for an 8-hour shift. Adding to the burden, the officer is personally encased in equipment; his panoply is cumbersome to walk in and irritating to sit down on. But the squad cab itself is full of even more "stuff." In the well between the seats, the cop might carry a clipboard, a flashlight, perhaps a cellular phone, and other administrative equipment. A computer monitor that ties him into the central criminal computer of the district and the city sits between the seats, oriented toward the driver.[1] At top and at bottom are controls for a traffic radar, sirens, and lights, including search lights that can extend to right, left, forward, or rear. Behind is the steel and Plexiglas screen that isolates the back of the squad where suspects are held.

All these structures and items are spatially constricting, but they are also tools of *freedom*. In his study of interstate truckers, Lawrence J. Ouellet (1990, p. 224) noted that the drivers' feeling of power on the road, of riding high on a big machine, was cited as the most important reason for holding the job. It is not illogical that a trucker feels freer cruising in an 18-wheel semi than in his family Saturn. Similarly, despite its confining atmosphere, a heavily armed squad car charged by a big engine, capable of hurtling through the streets with lights flashing and sirens screaming, yields a sense of power. Cops can make their presence *felt*. So, ironically, the same panoply that weighs down the police officer and narrows the size of his mobile office to less than that of the meanest airline seat also reminds him of his empowered separation from the rest of the population.

In addition, cops may define themselves by distinctions and differences of appearance, speech, belief, traditions, histories, membership, location, and assorted other, often minute, esoteric criteria and symbols. They also define themselves by who they are *not*. This can be a flexible boundary: Sometimes police will speak of "cops" as anyone in the department, from the chief to the detective, who wears a badge. Rarer still, they will include all workers in the legal system; occasionally the lowly, unarmed reserve officer in his or her light blue shirt is added. But the street officer himself is essentially the only one who can consistently claim permanent membership. In general, the "we" is the uniformed patrol officer; the "they" is everyone else. That does not mean cops are or view themselves as homogeneous; to the contrary, there are cliques of various kinds, friendship dyads, and other clusters of closer association between cops within the "patrol officer" grouping. But the major divisions of reference are between cop and public (Sacks, 1972; Van Maanen, 1978a). Because cops see themselves as the point men of law enforcement, they take pride as insiders but often act and think like outsiders (surrounded by potential enemies and others who do not understand them). As is generally the case, positive attachment to a group is shown to increase one's identification with its standards and practices (Redl, 1942; Sherif & Cantril, 1947). Essentially, then, the primary loyalty of an officer is to his comrades in the trenches, the buddy on the beat, and his station house colleagues.

Propinquity is one of the bases for the camaraderie of any group (Clark, 1972, p. 59; Secord & Backman, 1964, p. 39; cf. Festinger, Schachter, & Back, 1963; Whyte, 1943). Cops, who, after all, spend their professional lives with other cops, fit this distinction well. Although they cruise alone (in SLP, at least), they are in physical proximity when they take a call together or arrive to back each other up. Roll call, lunch, booking, seminars, the locker room, and meeting on the street all afford opportunities for contact. Sanctifying and justifying each other's decisions in the field are one main unit of discourse. Cops thus are an extended support group for each other, although the dialogue involves much more rough talk than would be allowed at a codependent's meeting. More important, cops share the same troubles and triumphs, speak a common argot, and are "there" for the same events. The analogy to a family is strong (see Jeanjean, 1990). Extravocational contacts also facilitate the bonding experience: Cops are friends with other cops. In the SLP Police Department (SLP-PD), cop buddies or groups would work out at the gym, go on fishing trips, or even start side businesses together. The centripetal forces strengthening group solidarity are many and ubiquitous.

This bonding is reinforced by outsiders' stereotyping of cops. Their uniform denotes their occupational role but also who they are, not just the job but also the mind, character, and probable behavior of the man or woman in the uniform. Cops, whose vocation and survival depend on profiling the public, believe that they too are profiled. The characteristics of the profile—for the beat cop, stupidity; for all cops, a tendency toward violence—are commonly portrayed on television. When cops in the ethnography talked about how the public acquired impressions about them, TV was always cited as the source. Whether these profiles are in fact correct is an unanswerable question. But the basic point is that cops believe that when they show up, people look at them and see a cop, not a human being but someone in a uniform, and in the same way that they are seen as representative of all cops, all cops represent them. Cops can be seen as fitting a definition of *minority:* "any group of people who because of the physical or cultural characteristics are singled out from others in the society in which they live for differential and unequal treatment" (Wirth, 1945, p. 347). Cops feel that they are differentiated and get unequal treatment once they don their physically distinctive "skin" of navy blue. Like any minority group, they face "antis" and "philos," people who hold negative prejudices against them because they are cops and people who hold positive prejudices. All, they would say, feel some sort of prejudice, and that in itself is important, for groups are sustained by how they are viewed as a group, as one standing for all and all being summed up by one.

The negative aspect of this struggle of definition is another enforcer of group solidarity. *PP:* "A fellow cop can let you down but he probably won't stab you in the back." Groups define themselves in opposition to or in conflict with other groups. Thus, one may have a positive attachment to one reference group but a negative attachment to another. This is reinforced every time a young man in handcuffs shouts, "Fucking cops!" at any blue uniform in sight. Indeed, conflict, instead of being dysfunctional, can be an "integrative force in the group" (Simmel, 1955, p. 17; cf. Coser, 1956). The group, finding itself in a situation of actual or perceived danger, bonds closer—the "circle the wagons" effect (Clark, 1972, pp. 87-88). In wartime, research has shown, soldiers are motivated to work, fight, kill, and even die not as much for patriotism or abstract causes as for loyalty to their immediate reference group of buddies (Shils, 1950). In times of life-and-death struggles (e.g., war, rebellion, disaster) between groups, the black-and-white distinction will be sharpest and bitterest. With cops, it is the inherent but potential dangers of violence that breed caution about the trustworthiness of noncops. In general, it is cops versus the mean world.

EVERYONE IS INNOCENT

Meanness does not necessarily translate as violence or potential violence; much of it arises from the seeming duplicity of ordinary folks—the lies discussed previously. That cops live in a mean world strangely does not register with the public in one very important way—people do not understand why cops should be suspicious of them or not believe that they are the exceptions to the rule. "They think we're idiots," a cop says to me, shaking his head. By this he largely refers to the situation in which an ordinarily law-abiding person, a noncriminal type, has in fact committed a violation of the law. All these good people—who in a film noir are usually dubbed the "law-abiding taxpayers"—have good excuses. The woman was speeding because she was late for work, and "my child's been sick and I've been late a lot. If I'm late again, they'll fire me." A man has expired tags on his car. "Oh, they're sitting at home on top of my refrigerator, and I've been forgetting to put 'em on. But I do have them!" A man scores a 1.7 on the Breathalyzer but begs, "Officer, I live a couple of blocks from here. Just let me go home. I made one mistake." A teenager is caught shoplifting. "My friend must have put it in my pocket as a joke. I didn't do it!" A man hits another car head-on in a parking lot, then speeds away. This is witnessed, and an officer catches the suspect at a stoplight a few blocks from the crime scene. The man looks incredulous. "Did I hit somebody? Oh my God, you're right, I did. I'm sorry, officer, I didn't even notice." These are the mundane excuses. A more complex defense is that of the man with an outstanding traffic warrant who says he cannot afford to pay the fine because his little daughter is dying of cancer and he is spending all his money on the hospital bills. I never encountered the proverbial husband rushing his suspiciously slender-waisted wife to the delivery room, but I did meet a couple who looked rather vibrant and healthy despite their 80 mile-an-hour rush to dialysis.

What is a cop to do when presented with these late 20th-century pardon tales? Everyone has an excuse, everyone is innocent, and no one really deserves a ticket or an arrest. But what is particularly interesting here, I think both to cops who live the experience and to the ethnographer who observes it and to some extent internalizes it, is that whether people are lying or not, they really seem to expect that their pleas and protests should be accepted at face value. This is probably based partly on people's self-perception that they are generally good and should not be punished for a one-time offense. That they may have been speeding to work every day—committing the offense many times but never having been caught—is not enumerated either in the excuse or their rationalization of it. The feeling is, "I am not a criminal, and thus my technical violation of the law must be excused or expunged because it is inconsistent with my character." But to the cop, who has heard thousands on thousands of such statements, two messages are decoded from their quantity and sincere quality. The first is that the offender really does think the cop is an idiot. An officer could reasonably ask, "Do you really think that I should not write a ticket for anyone with a good excuse? Should I call your work and talk to your boss? Check the list of dialysis patients? Go home with you to get those tags and help you put them on?" The cop hears the explanations every day; the usually law-abiding citizen has perhaps one such encounter per lifetime. It is a collision of expectations, assumptions, and ego validation.

The link to the TV cop was often commented on. The TV cop is omniscient, we all are aware. His hunch cracks the case; his sudden recollection of a detail of someone's testimony brings about the final resolution. But if TV cops know, then why do people lie to real cops? "They expect us to be mind-readers," one cop tells me, "like Kojak, or something." The context is a car stop, with another sensible and sentimental proffered excuse: "I'm late for my daughter's birthday party." The cop scoffs, *PP:* "Maybe the guy was late for his daughter's party, but so what? I'm supposed to know this? And if I confirm, does that mean everyone who has a reason to speed, because he's late for something, should be allowed to speed? They expect me to know that they're a good person and so I guess they think that good people should be allowed to speed." Another cop similarly reasons, "They think if they're white and middle class and church-goers, then it's okay for them to break the law when they want to or really need to." Another cop adds, "We're supposed to, like, wave our priests' hands or something and say, well, okay, break the law, that's fine, just this one time, 'cause you're obviously a nice guy." And finally, "They think we're a dumb street cop and maybe we're too stupid to know that they're lying," but on the other hand, "they expect us to sense" their good hearts.

Whereas the citizen seems to think that admitting to a crime makes him or her a criminal, the cop's perspective is simply that an unlawful act has been committed. Cops know that good people speed. But the accused public's perpetual excuses contribute to the general cynicism and doubt of police officers for the veracity of everyone they meet, whatever their status, race, or demeanor. Even the most inebriated partygoer, unable on repeated tries to find the nose on his own face, will deny that he is drunk. Protestations of innocence are standard and made by people who in ordinary circumstances may be reasonably honest. If only "hard" criminals lied to them, cops would be less cynical: But everyone, not just the proverbial murderers and rapists, contributes to the meanness of the cop's world.

It is worth exploring the nature of public mendacity about their own status and its commonplace occurrence. People may, for example, lie about their identity. Teens especially will, when at a car stop or when found engaging in a suspicious activity, give a false name. What is astounding and dismally humorous about such lies is how easily they are uncovered. Teens will claim to have no ID, perhaps illogically expecting the cop to shrug and cease to pursue the issue. They do not foresee being held until their ID is established, especially in car stop situations. Or even more strangely, they will lie about their identity one moment, then provide their real name in response to another question. Lies, as many sages have cautioned, are difficult to sustain, spontaneous lies especially. The cop, unfortunately for the suspect, takes the lie as an affront to his intelligence. One cop sums up the attitude with this declaration: "Never trust anybody under 17."

People also lie about their criminal records. I noted the following interchange after a car stop. The cop and I sat in the front of the cruiser. A teenage boy sat in the back and peeped through the open slot in the partition. The cop had the boy's license in hand, fingers poised above the onboard computer.

Cop, *PP:* Do you have any prior moving violations, any tickets?
Teen: No, man, no.
Cop: You're sure?
Teen: I'm clean, man.
Cop: So if I run your license now, I won't find anything?
Teen: Nope.
Cop: Nope what?
Teen: No, I'm clean.
Cop: You have no prior tickets, no DUI, no citations?
Teen: Clean. Look at it.
Cop: I am. I just wanted to ask you first. You aren't lying to me?
Teen: No, you know, I don't have nothing. Nothing at all.

The crinkle in the officer's lip betrays his estimate of the young man's candor. He runs the license; the computer brings up screen after screen of citations for reckless driving, broken taillights, failures to heed stop signs and traffic lights, two DUIs, and so on.

Teen: Oh, man, that stuff!
Cop: You forgot about it?
Teen: That was nothing, you know.
Cop: I know.

Faced with the lies of the public, the cop struggles to define his own identity. One cop asserts, "The TV detective—of course he knows what is gonna happen. He's read the script!" And, "When they're not lying, people expect us to know it. When they lie, they expect us not to know it." Each officer with whom I rode or spoke at some point mentioned the differences between the TV cop's omniscience and his or her own lived experience; the distinctions are less in type than degree. The street cop does have hunches about guilt and innocence, about who is lying and who is telling the truth. Street pardons are granted; mercy is bestowed. But it is their perception that the public, bombarded by images of "smart-ass TV detectives," assumes that cops are either brilliant mind readers or empaths or callous, stupid jerks. The public's self-perception of essential innocence interplays with this binary stereotype of the cop and results in the automatic response of the pardon tale and the protest of innocence. The street cop does not deny the egotistical nature of the human psyche as a factor but again sees the octopus-like tentacle of TV's influence crowding, pushing, and interfering with his daily practice. Behind every lie, protestation, and tall tale is the shadow of mass media.

NO RESPECT FROM THE AUDIENCE

If police often feel dissatisfied with the return for the energy that they have expended or feel that they are being called on to engage in duties that go unrewarded in today's legal system and social climate, then what would make them happy? The question is not as trite as it seems. Obviously, the dramaturgical metaphor fails literally in the realm of the ultimate audience reaction that a stage performer seeks: applause. Police work, with its varieties of conduct and situations, does not lend itself to applause in application. However, a simple "Thank you, officer" uttered with sincerity, not sarcasm, is genuinely appreciated. Most cops are working-class men and women who would experience discomfort at a florid emotional response from those they attempt to protect and serve.

The mean world can be triggered by associations with events and persons that hardly seem to conjure meanness; this is a signifier that the cop's world is not ours. Riding along one day, we were called to a matchbook house in a poorer residential neighborhood. I recorded the incident in my notes:

> An eviction. . . . Two officers called, including Jake, my ride. Kay is also there in another squad [Kay was one of only two female officers]. The landlord is a little old lady, fat, hobbled by arthritis. The house is immaculate, with cat figurines, a giant spoons-of-the-world wall panel, and a picture of a blond, moist-eyed Jesus. The tenant is male, 30ish, and white, with a crafty face, sharp nose, and darting eyes; he is edgy—as if on drugs. She tells us that he has refused to pay rent and has threatened her physically. They are stereotypes of victim and villain! The officers have dealt with the guy before; Kay later tells me he made sexual cracks to her [in a previous encounter]. He sits in a chair facing Jake and the other officers, basically blaming everything on the old lady. He says her daughter threatened him. Jake tells him over and over that he has to leave the house. The man starts loading up his stuff into a car. The old lady is afraid of him. . . . Jake motions for her to let him handle it. She tells me she doesn't like to take in tenants but must for financial reasons. Her husband, a veteran . . . died 30 years ago. She mentions a daughter. Jake comments, "We bluffed him out—sometimes justice is swift." Duress under color of law: Old woman felt threatened; bad guy is bounced. In tears the woman grasps Jake's hand, but Jake refuses to let me take their picture.

It was a photograph, however, that no public relations-conscious police department would object to: an old lady gratefully clasping the hand of the cop, emotionally thanking him for his service. But significantly Jake told me later, "I didn't want to embarrass her; it looked too good, too advertising."

But the incident had a coda of meanness. At the station for lunch hours later, Jake talked to another officer, Tony, a veteran, who said he remembered the old lady and that she used to live elsewhere and had a delinquent son. Jake experienced a flash of recognition. The woman's son passed out in a bar many years ago. Jake was called and tried to revive him. The son woke up and punched him. Then he was restrained and put in an ambulance. Because the man was potentially violent, the ambulance driver insisted a cop go with them. On the way to the hospital the ambulance crashed into another car. Jake was badly injured. Still on duty today, he is also partly on disability. During the rest of the shift, he shook his head over the irony of the encounter. Thus, a good act became part of a bad memory.

But cops do insist on an attitude and a tone of respect in their presence: "Contempt of cop" is a serious violation of the unwritten laws of the street. The decision to arrest someone is generally tempered by, among other factors, the level of respect shown to the uniformed officer (Black, 1970). The surly teenager, as said, is the chief violator of this injunction. What amazed me when listening to teenagers sass, sneer at, or practically laugh in the faces of police officers is how little fear they showed of the consequences of this sort of behavior. An older cop told me, "They used to be terrified of us. But they used to be even more scared of what their parents would say when we took 'em home. That used to be a way to get 'em. They'd beg us not to tell their dad what they did. Now they say, 'Wait 'til my mom finds out. Her boyfriend's a lawyer and he's gonna sue you.' " Many people are disrespectful to the police officers, most of all but certainly not exclusively teenagers. It is the context of the communication—who is exhibiting this offensive behavior—that is vital to understand. Again, in the moral universe of the cop, there are bad guys and there are good guys. The problem is that so many people who would ordinarily be classified as good guys become bad—to judge by their behavior and their words—in the presence of police officers. In the mean world of police work, truly good guys are rarely encountered, save as victims.

Several incidents highlighted the context of the phenomenon of disrespect to the officer. In a police department, like many extremely concerned—from the point of view of street officers, sometimes excessively concerned—with good community relations and paranoid about lawsuits, there were many times when the citizen seemed more in control of the situation than the officer. I witnessed a scene of which I produced no photograph because it probably would have exacerbated an already tense situation but whose audiovisual bitterness is indelibly printed in my brain. A raucous partygoer at a local hotel refused to leave after being told to do so by management. He spent half an hour—I know this, I checked my watch every 5 minutes—cursing the police, threatening them with lawsuits, boasting of his income, all while his mortified wife tried to silence him. The police endured it, I don't know why or how. After listening to that harangue for half an hour, almost any officer would have pardonably wished for a return to a time when cops had almost unlimited power in their own world. My *sotto voce* comment of exasperation to one of the officers summed up what I came to believe was an appropriate response: "Give me your nightstick. Let me beat him." And when my students asked me sometimes if I ever witnessed police brutality in SLP, I answered, half seriously, "Not enough."

Figure 6.2.

Disrespect may be shown physically as well as verbally; it can also be expressed in noncommunication—silence. Here, the surliness of teenagers is a common example. At another car stop, we pulled over four teens in what officers wryly called "Mommy's Mercedes." None was entitled to drive without a licensed driver in the car; all had learners' permits. The officer pulled out the driver. He was not drunk, but he was slouched, looking away. His friends were engaged in a giggly conversation, not treating this event with any seriousness. Their attitude was, "Hey, you can't really do anything to me." I think in such situations, a certain amount of class resentment may also exist. Those who traveled in Mommy's Mercedes, to judge them on the slimmest of evidence, were spoiled brats whose family lawyer could probably extricate them from any problem that was not already excused by their juvenile status. The surliness continued apace. The driver would not answer any questions; he was provokingly and silently smug. Then there was an abrupt transition. The officer grabbed him by the back of his collar and said very forcefully, inches from his face, "You will listen to me." The kid started; he behaved respectfully during the rest of the engagement.

Being ignored completely creates a paradoxical situation for the cop. Although he may at one moment object to living in a fishbowl—"What are those people looking at? They've never seen a cop before?"—in many circumstances he must command the public's attention to accomplish his duties. The man seated on the bench in Figure 6.2 was known to the cops as an alcoholic. Many times they had taken him to the Hennepin County detox unit or some other facility at which drunks were dropped off. From his appearance, he was severely inebriated. He also completely ignored the officers. They understood this; their verdict was, "He's out of it." However, their repeated efforts to negotiate him into the police car, to take him to an alcoholic unit, failed. He simply would not pay any attention. Finally, they had to handcuff him and take him away by force. In this instance, as well as in the car stop situation in which a driver was suspected of illegal levels of intoxication, ignoring the cop was taken as part of the foreseen pathology. *Not* to pay attention to a cop when he wants you to is a form of deviance but an excusable one in these cases because the violator is under diminished capacity. "Assholes" and surly teens do not merit this exemption.

Nor does disrespect occur only at the crime scene or call site. One of the most repeated and deplored instances in which the public fails to notice and instantly yield to the police is when a squad car goes to lights and sirens. In SLP, as elsewhere, when a police car is on a call with lights flashing and sirens blaring, the proper etiquette is for other motorists to get out of the way. In the older model of Crown Victoria, which was the police car the department used for about half of my ethnography, the sirens and wailers were built into the roof.[2] Outside the car, both kinds of sirens produced noises loud enough to be heard for miles, it seemed to me; on today's roads, however, the sirens' piercing shriek is challenged by the immovable object of the motorist with windows up, radio blasting, and mind drifting off to the day at the office.

I discovered four species of motorist as classified by their reaction to a cop car going to lights and sirens. First, there is the obedient driver who pulls as far as he can to the side of the road and slows down or stops to let the police car go by. Then, in progression of increasing irritation, there is the idler, who seems to take forever to pull aside and does so halfway and haltingly, obviously ready to speed up the instant the police car pulls parallel or passes by. The second vexing creature is the driver who does not notice the police car until it almost, to use a common phrase, "rides up his butt." Only then does he pull away, sometimes in panic, almost careening off the street. Finally, most perplexingly, and thankfully most rarely, there are the drivers who refuse to pull over at all, even though they are obviously watching the police in the rearview mirror. I have joined with cops in an adrenaline-induced fury at people in this last category. Not properly ceding the right of way to police officers is one more sign that the public fails to respect them, to give them their proper deference and due.

The relationship to the televisual portrayal of cop work is relevant. One officer made the following statement:

> On TV, cops, detectives, whatever, they get frustrated, but most of the time they get their way. I don't know whether you wanna do a study on this or something, but on the action shows, the real-life cop shows, it seems to me they almost always get their man, and the whole show is about them doing that. Everybody is paying attention to them.

I asked him, "When you walk into a room, do you want people to drop everything and instantly pay attention to you?" He smiled and said that he did not expect the whole world to pay attention to him all the time just because he was a cop, but he could offer solutions to problems and, after all, almost always was there because someone had called him, somebody wanted him to be there, to help. Once he is on stage, especially when summoned by the public, the cop *must* command attention.

Sometimes officers are much less understanding of the circumstances of their being ignored. It was late one night, and we got a "loud party" call at a local hotel. We arrived at a rented room that was jam-packed with 20- and 30-somethings. It was the tail end of a wedding party that had become informal and raucous; neckties had all been shed, and there was no tuxedo shirt without Velveeta or beer stains on it. The officer I was riding with arrived at the same time as his backup. We entered the room; everyone was dancing, paying scant attention to the arrival of the police. All denied that it was their party. Several of the men started laughing, not taking the incident seriously, the next step up in disrespect for an officer. The lead cop literally moved center stage and tried to turn off the stereo. There was a moment's hesitation; he could not find the power switch. It would have been an embarrassing scene if he had failed, but he found it, the music was cut off, and he boomed out that the party was over. All eyes were immediately on him. He had taken control; he had seized attention. Once a marginal player on the stage, he was now the star, determining the plot's progression.

THE SYSTEM IS AGAINST THEM:
STATISTICS AS BULLSHIT

No street cop I ever spoke to had complete faith in the system, even though they were its most prominent enforcers; they believed that punishment would rarely ever fit the crime committed by those they apprehended. There is a context to this perspective: Police see (and feel and smell) crime and its results as no one else does, except the perpetrators and the victims. They are in self-perception the authentic or real parts of the system from which other parts only capture echoes or palimpsest impressions. To achieve knowledge about the crime, superiors, lawyers, and everyone else in the legal system must borrow narratives and descriptions from cops. One cop put it this way: *PP:* "Once a perp gets to court and is shaved, cleaned up, and coached by a lawyer, he's not the same man, nor is the crime as well understood in retrospect." He insisted, "Everybody depends on us; they read our notes to find out what happened."[3] The full horror of the crime and true nature of criminals never make their full impact on the system. The crooks, then, "never get what they deserve" (i.e., justice that truly punishes the crime).

The show must go on, however. The failure of the system may embitter a police officer and affect his work, but he is still on stage and must perform each night for the audience. A key understanding to the motivation for their behavior is that the men and women in uniform, the embodiment of authority and law, the guardians of the thin blue line, believe that they are rebels and that to some extent the offenders they arrest are those in real power. A teen in an expensive sports car was given a ticket for having illegally dark windshield glass. Walking away, the cop heard him loudly snort to his girlfriend in the passenger seat, "My dad'll have this fixed, no problem." The cop told me about it in the car. The teen's dad was a big-shot lawyer who probably would get the record expunged somehow. "I knew that when I wrote the ticket," said the officer. Likewise, although the cop knows that a burglar may never do serious time, or that the lawyer will plead down the charge, or that the judge will reduce any length of sentence (and most prisons are too crowded to keep people for their full term), that does not mean that he should give up on acting out his part. In some way, in expressing this attitude—"the system is screwed up, but I'm still gonna do my job"—cops echo the "oath-bound" guardsmen of Yeats's decaying *Black Tower,* whose king is dead and whose cause is lost but who still fight the enemies who come "to bribe or threaten." Being one of the only cogs in the wheel of justice that does good or tries to do good enhances the cop's status as outsider from that very system and validates (and valorizes) his own view of his motivations for being a cop.

The enhancement of outsider status from being "there" and having insider knowledge is perpetuated by the cop's attitude toward the realm of knowledge about police work other than the televisual: statistics. It is here where ethnography and other research methods such as social surveys or content analyses or even critical interpretations of media contexts break sharply. The duty of the ethnographer is to approximate, appreciate, and translate, by word and image, the world she or he has observed. The complication in evaluating police work is that it is very difficult to produce any sort of baseline from which to compare or contrast cop perceptions of street reality. It is for this reason that I have defined street reality as the way cops see reality. I found this largely to be the way that I myself saw and interpreted the incidents I witnessed. I have attempted here in my description of previous research—especially in the content of television and, to some extent, my descriptions of police perceptions of crime rates, for example—to relate these to so-called "official" statistics about crime. The irony lies in the fact that these statistics are in essence held by the officers to be, to put it bluntly, bullshit. They do not believe in statistics, but they are often judged by them (Manning, 1977). Police resentment of the use of numerical evaluation stems from their view that the measure is crude, confusing "good" and "bad" police work, and is seen as a managerial ploy on the part of police supervisors to control and speed up work in the field.[4]

The first reason for doubting crime statistics is that police are aware of how little crime enters the indices through their own efforts. An example is a domestic assault. In a typical case, an officer is called to a house or an apartment based on a complaint lodged by a neighbor or by someone living within.

According to Minnesota law, domestic assault is no longer a charge to be filed by the individual citizen; the arrest should be made by the officer if he has reason to suspect that physical violence has taken place. This, incidentally, is another area in which officers are assisted in the performance of their duty by public ignorance of the law. They will ask the victim (almost always a woman), "Did he hit you? Did he strike you in any way?" She may very well have no interest in her husband or partner being taken to jail. "By the time we've shown up, a lot of times they've sobered up, even begun to reconcile." She may want the officer simply to talk to the male, straighten him out, give him a warning—justice, not law, is requested. Legally, the officer is interested in one thing: Was there violence? She may offer a "Yes, but . . ." or "Yes, he hit me, but it wasn't much." Or she will say, "Yes, he hit me, but I know he didn't mean it and we were arguing," and so on. The "yes" is the trigger word. The man is going to jail; nothing she will say or do at this point will alter that inevitable fate. The officer may also look for evidence, a bruise or welt. "Did he do that to you?" or, "That looks pretty recent. Where'd you get that?"

That is the procedure. In practice, the officers are well aware of several conditions that skew any statistical appreciation of the statewide or even nationwide rate of domestic assault. First, they do not get called in every case. The "it's not my business" rule of crime reporting applies everywhere, not just New York City. The concerned neighbor may not call; the wife may not call; no one may call. So the cops do not come. There is no way to tell, then, whether the domestic assaults that they are called to investigate are the tip of the iceberg or the majority. Second, on the arrival of cops, people can sober up. A bruise may not be visible, or a wife may deny or be in a state of denial. Especially if she has had experience with the cops, she may know the consequences of saying she was hit. Again, the result may be that no charge is filed, and therefore no statistic is generated. Third, although the weight of the law pushes the officer toward making an arrest, the fact remains that it is his judgment call. Is the woman lying just to punish her husband? Is the bruise really fresh? Is she concealing something; should she be compelled to talk? The chasm between what an officer feels, senses, or assumes and what he can prove may be narrow or canyonesque. It also diminishes the number of crimes and alleged crimes that enter "the books." In essence, crime is edited to fit the communication formats of the law enforcement system (Shearing & Ericson, 1991).

Crime rates are also, as cops know, a product of changes in department policy or public pressure (see DeFleur, 1975). The great emphasis on rooting out domestic assailants, for example, is a recent phenomenon. But more localized mandates can also skew crime statistics wildly. For instance, at roll call, the shift sergeant might announce that a particular stretch of street or highway is the subject of citizen complaints. Naturally, it will be more closely watched by officers seeking traffic offenders. Regardless of the merit of the original complaints, more people will be pulled over, and thus very likely more will be charged with a vehicle offense of some kind, ranging from driving under the influence to expired license tags. "Get-tough" policies of various kinds, targeted toward various offenses, would, by this mechanism, invariably produce more arrests for the targeted location and type of crime. Because, as cops believe, there is some crime everywhere, it is no surprise to them that they can find it when they are told where to look for it. In this sense, "getting tough" is a self-confirming action.

Another reason that cops' credence in crime statistics is irresolute is that they know how the same event can be recategorized by the legal system through the machinations of lawyers and the exigencies of the law. As Alan Dershowitz (1983) noted, almost all his clients, or any defense attorney's clients for that matter, are guilty, meaning they have committed the crimes for which they are accused in a court of law or have committed offenses that approximately correspond to the charges as filed. Yet Dershowitz claims that this is both morally untroubling and socially unproblematic: "I do not apologize for (or feel guilty about) helping let a murderer go free" (p. xvi). This is because his duty is to serve the client, not justice. In commenting on this defense of the legal system by lawyers, linguist Deborah Tannen (1998) argues that the system of ruthless partisanship, excluding truth and justice and humanity, "disrupts human impulses toward honesty and corrupts human relationships. This is hurtful to the human spirit" (p. 148). It is particularly hurtful to the spirit of those—such as police officers—who must serve both justice and the law.

These variations play out on the street. A man was stopped on the highway. His late-model Continental was weaving and bucking. When the officer ran the tag, he found a long string of traffic and DUI offenses. The man was red-faced and angry at the cop, spitting out a version of the old saw, "Why aren't you out there catching rapists and murderers? Why are you bothering me?" He had had only a couple of drinks, he claimed. He could hardly walk a straight line or touch his nose on the street exam. In the car, he failed the Breathalyzer test. In the station, he registered a full point above the legal limit. He was charged; he called a lawyer and was bailed out rapidly. Six months later, in conversation, a cop brought him up as an example of a drunk driver who wasn't. He worked out a deal, paid a huge fine, and got his case expunged. So, although he *was* a drunk driver, he never entered the books as such. People break the law regularly, but it is a tortuous process to have the state declare that they are lawbreakers. This is a dichotomy that has yet to be accounted for in mass communication research: Cops have a good case that the world is much, much meaner than official statistics attest.

Another problem with the truth value of statistics, cops understand, is that there is a subjective, selective element to who is detected, apprehended, and arrested, as well as who is convicted (Black, 1970; Ericson, 1982). Here, police officers can be much more sophisticated than criminologists. An example I observed was the car stop. Even on the darkest night of the northern plains winter, there are always some cars on the road, any of which an officer on patrol can

choose to stop. It is a joke among cops that every car has some violation to target if one wanted to. Who gets stopped? Gender plays a role. A cop is much less
likely to stop a woman with a mob of tots in a station wagon. This is less mercy
than pragmatism: "What are you going to do with those kids if you end up having to take her in?" Class also plays a role. The old, rusted-out tin can junker's
plates are run much more often than those of the middle-class, well-washed
Buick. The role of race is trickier. I never once heard an officer say, "Hey, that's
a black guy. Let's run his plates." It was more likely that if the black guy's
plates were run it was because he was in a junker, late at night, with a taillight
out. In any case, cops know that they cannot be statistical samplers, taking
some sort of random estimate of the population of cars that pass by. They have
to play hunches. Society may legitimately debate on what basis such profile
hunches should be made, but the input of the officer whose lived experience
has taught him what to expect should not be invalidated by those who demand
politically desirable abstractions. The officer knows, however, that in essence
he is being subjective.

In deciding who to arrest and who goes to jail, statistics fail again according
to the street cop and others. Civil libertarians and antipolice activists might be
amazed at some of the comments that I heard from gruff, veteran, politically
reactionary street cops. "That guy's gonna end up in jail, and it's only for one
reason: 'cause he's black. A jury would never send a white man to jail for the
same crime." Or, *PP:* "That kid will do community service 'cause he's a privileged, white suburbanite who probably lives three doors down from the judge."
Such comments about race and class were frequent. One detective described to
me a white-collar crime that he had investigated. The legal case ended with a
deal between the attorney general's office and the accused's lawyers. A fine
was paid, a lesser charge pleaded. "The guy stole millions and he's scott-free
and still rich and driving a Mercedes." I paraphrase his conclusion: "If he was a
poor black kid who knocked over a liquor store for a hundred bucks, he'd be in
prison for a couple years, even if he didn't hurt anybody and his gun wasn't
loaded." I will not exaggerate the importance of such comments by claiming
that the officers I spoke to are liberal humanists in navy blue. Rather, they are
completely aware of the subjective nature of law enforcement. Where their
opinions differ from a more liberal stance on crime and law enforcement is that
their lamentations tend to be about who *doesn't* go to jail rather than who does.
Whatever subjectivity they practice pales when compared to the mysterious
and, I think they will argue, socially fatal system of plea bargaining, where a
murder becomes a misdemeanor, a drunken assault is dismissed, a string of
thefts is traded away for testimony against another thief, and so on.

Finally, statistics fail to measure the good that cops do in qualitative ways,
that is, in the function of guardian of the peace. In the eviction of the potentially
violent tenant cited earlier, the cops had solved a problem for a little old lady.
Despite the later recrudescence of a bad associated memory, the cop had
accomplished a good deed. No tick book would catalog such a maneuver, nor

would it register a heart-to-heart with an angry teenager who gave him something to think about besides his own anomie. Unenumerated as well are moments of simply helping people—giving directions to a lost tourist or helping a kid straighten out his bike tire. Nor are positive interactions that perpetuate a good image of cops noted in the statistical record (see Figure 1.2). When, for example, a cop collects some hubcaps that neighborhood kids have found strewn on the street, he spends 10 minutes inventorying them, entering data into the department's records. But absent from the books is his joking around with the kids during that span of time, about how they had "broken a big hubcap ring" and should "consider joining the FBI."

More important, as we drove away from the hubcap scene and the kids were smiling and waving, no camera, not even my own, was able to fully capture the pleasant interaction and its amiable closure. The officer mentioned as an aside, "Where's *Cops* when you need them?" This was a frequent caption to much of the "good" that cops did, although, as I have noted, ironically, they felt some embarrassment when I tried to capture such instances with the camera. On television, the good and the bad that mass-mediated cops, whether detectives or, more rarely, uniformed officers, enact are entered into the public record in the most spectacular way, for it is viewed by millions on their television sets. The cop patrolling the streets in the real world typically has the smallest of audiences. Only his brother and sister cops may ever learn of the exploits, and even in those cases, the laconic nature of their conversations and their natural modesty forbid boasting except in jest. So, as another cop put it, *PP:* "On TV, they get credit for everything. Here, we only get credit for something that can go into the crime statistics." There is no sourness in his complaint, but it does register that the mass media cop has certain advantages in her or his competition with the street cop.

TALES OF DECLINE

A binding agent in any group is the shared traditions of the group's history. Such socialization is cited as occurring early in a rookie's training, reaching back to the academy where "group think," a "we-they" separation of cop versus world, is impressed by instructors and reinforced by " 'war stories' and corridor anecdotes" (Bahn, 1984, p. 392). Disseminating memories, real and projected, of "past days" is also one way that the tension of modern police work is both exacerbated and relieved. Cops remind each other how scary the world is but, in doing so, assure each other that their comrades are "in the same boat." In the SLP-PD, there was no palpable sense of history that would be recognized by a Serbian still inspired by the medieval battle of Kosovo—that is, no deep-rooted common folktale attuned to specific persons, places, and events that defined the group's shared memory. In fact, the history of the department, which stretched back to the late 19th century, was largely unknown to almost every officer I spoke to. Only one old sergeant on the verge of retirement had spent time investigating the subject and rescued some old archives and logbooks from oblivion. Neither did the fraternal banter between officers or the corporate rhetoric of the department stress specific events. Rather, historical memory played a defining role for the SLP-PD community through tales from old fields. Older officers told younger officers about "the way things used to be."

This dynamic was actually part of the training process of the rookie officers by the veteran officer (their field training officer, or FTO). As Van Maanen (1978b) found in one of his studies of the new rookie, and I observed as well, the FTO-rookie relationship was as much retraining as training. Veteran cops tell the rookies what they know. The advice is often practical. *PP:* "You notice how that car has white steam blowing out of the exhaust pipe?" In Minnesota in January, it is an unmistakable sign that the car has just been started. But veteran officers (not just the FTO) also impart the culture of cynicism and suspicion that, I have argued, is a survival trait and only becomes dysfunctional *in extremis.* Within tales of paranoia and moral rot come reminiscences. I never heard anyone use the expression "the good old days," but they generally referred to a time before quack psychologists and "liberal fuckhead" sociologists demoralized crime, before the lawyers "perverted" the legal system, and a time when, as Mike Royko once put it in a famous column, newspapermen were from the same class as cops and were even the sons of cops so they really understood what cop work was like (Gutmann, 1993).

In short, the old days were better: These are tales that fit into a general pattern of older persons talking about the past in the "voice of decline" (Beauregard, 1993). The degeneration in the state of public behavior toward the police is set at the 1970s in the wake of the social upheaval and changes of the 1960s.[5] An interesting spillover of this voice is that new cops adopt the standard; they rarely speak in terms of "the old days" as if they were there, but they are able to relate the general erosion of the autonomy of the cop and the decline in the law-abiding nature of the public.[6] It is a similar phenomenon to that explored by Kasinitz and Hillyard (1995) in the neighborhood of Red Hook, New York, where "old-timers" voiced disapproval of the present and nostalgia about the past, especially about crime and the behavior of young people. The researchers suggest that by

> speaking the language of loss . . . they also give the newcomers, who take up the nostalgic imagery, an effective political tool. The old-timers themselves are generally fatalistic about their community. Yet, although nostalgia can provide grounds for fatalism, it can also become a resource with which actors claim authenticity and the right to define the "community" in the future. (Kasinitz & Hillyard, 1995, p. 162)

It also provided a linchpin to define their community as one that, in essence, is under siege by a wider world that does not uphold the values they cherish, which in their worldview are the authentic traditional values of policing.[7]

Figure 6.3.

Media portrayals of police officers emphasize violence, in which force and trickery are the main tools that cops use to solve problems and to get people to do what they want them to do. For the SLP cops, rhetorical strategies took precedence over physical manipulation, although obviously the implied threat of an armed police officer may in itself be an intimidating factor. One aspect of police work that I was unprepared for, however, one that was the subject of much discussion with the cops, was how they felt that the public was less intimidated by them, less likely to follow their commands than in previous eras. An older cop put it this way: "They used to do what you told them to do. People used to be afraid of us. Now they laugh in our faces, especially the kids. They know juvenile law or they think they know juvenile law." A detective noted, *PP:* "They pick up the jargon from TV about technicalities and what's covered under the law. Some of it's bullshit, but it does make them think that they're immune. They're much less intimidated by police than they were 20 years ago."

Obviously, from the point of view of police, the lack of intimidation is dysfunctional; it makes their job more dangerous, less efficient. There is more likelihood of their role being upstaged, of public embarrassment, or of their star performance being undermined by a criminal, a suspect, or anyone who refuses to follow the script the officer would like to play out. The man struggling with cops, shown in Figure 6.3, was found drunk on the street after an "out-of-control" party. He assaulted an officer and then ran away, only later to stop and give himself up.[8] He unleashed a torrent of abuse on the officers, teaching me several expletives of which I was previously unaware. The counterstrategy of the police varied. Some laughed in amusement and ignored his antics while continuing to take him in for booking. The cop who had received the brunt of the man's abuse, however, tried to be physically intimidating, to grab the man, to threaten him. The man was too drunk to care or to understand. He refused to cooperate. He had to be dragged back to the jail cells. After the incident, a younger cop repeated the phrase that is almost a slogan of the officers: "In the old days, it wouldn't have happened that way." If encounters with violent, abusive members of the citizenry reinforce cops' suspicion and cynicism, they also provide evidence for tales of decline in the value of their work and of society itself. The coda: The man in the picture later was arrested and convicted of stabbing another police officer with a knife.

CONCLUSIONS: REBELS AGAINST THE PUBLIC?

It is ironic that police, the ultimate symbol of authority, consider themselves to some extent to be rebels. On one hand, people expect the cop to be a hero. On the other, there is a tremendous reservoir of cynicism about his or her abilities that immediately finds expression when the hero function is unfulfilled. Police work is a study in the contradiction between such expectations and reality. In particular there is tension inherent in asking cops to serve and protect but also to monitor and regulate the citizenry (Denyer, Callender, & Thompson, 1975; Greene, 1989). The through-the-squad-windshield world is indeed mean and dangerous, but cops must also "relate" to that same community. Most crucially, the uniformed cop is, as mentioned earlier, often the bringer of bad news, the gatekeeper of the unsatisfying and impersonal criminal justice system (Regoli, Poole, & Hewitt, 1979).

To some extent, then, cops are rebels *against* the public, although at the same time they "protect and serve" them. It is impossible for cops to endure innumerable encounters in which they are verbally and physically abused by the public without developing a great degree of cynicism about the population in general and thus also perhaps overestimate general criminality. Certainly, such unease is manifested in public attitudes toward law enforcement and crime. Researchers have noted a decline in the mythology of "state sovereignty," that government "is capable of providing security, law, and order, and crime control within its territorial boundaries" (Garland, 1996, p. 448; see also Hirst, 1994; Lash & Urry, 1987). It is an important and disturbing phenomenon that those in charge of guarding the citizenry have in some sense lost faith in their own role. Historically, after all, democracies fail when the guardians and guarded feel that "freedom" is no longer worth the price of personal fear. It is socially dysfunctional for cops to feel that they are guarding the Black Tower, no matter how diligent their service or how seriously they feel bound by their oaths.

Again, such overestimation is a survival strategy. Those who regulate the police system or critique it, whether in the academy, in police administration, or in the press, are asking police to engage in suicidal activity if they do not employ some degree of stereotyping, including racial stereotyping, and distrust. And perhaps it is the police who see the statistical truth. Every year, tens of thousands of violent crimes go unsolved, which means that cumulatively, over decades, there are millions of potentially dangerous citizens populating our mean world, and, especially, the world of cops. The average time served in jail for murder in the United States is only 8 years. For more minor offenses, including major crimes of violence, offenders serve lesser sentences, are released because of prison overcrowding, or escape incarceration altogether. It may be that the public citizen who does *not* see a murderer around every corner is fooling herself or himself. It is obviously in the interests of the higher powers— mayors and police chiefs—to obscure this reality. Patrol officers, however, must walk among it every day and survive to the end of the shift. It is true, then, that in the front stage, cops are "heavy viewers" of meanness, but, by some measures, it really is a mean and scary world after all.

NOTES

1. SLP cars are laid out for a single officer to drive alone. The rider—in this case myself—is allowed about half the sitting area of that in a normal vehicle; I would often be forced to sit, along with my camera bag, in a contorted position. Sometimes an officer would put aside the shotgun, seen prominently at right of Figure 6.1, to give me more room.

2. They were, without exaggeration, deafening. The ears ached, and conversation was strained and difficult; I didn't see how anyone could ignore the onslaught. A newer model car was introduced with the sirens wisely placed in the front grille. This considerably lessened the interior noise.

3. Geertz (1973) stated, "The culture of a people is an ensemble of texts, themselves ensembles, which the anthropologist strains to read over the shoulder of those to whom they properly belong" (p. 452).

4. Street cops are concerned with the use of numerical figures in determining police effectiveness (Smith & Gray, 1983, pp. 56-61). There is a front-stage/back-stage dichotomy here as well, of course. City officials, presidents, policymakers, journalists, academics, and all other denizens of the legal system use and abuse such statistics, point to and deny them, and replicate and reinforce them, as if they are the crucial evidence of the true picture of law enforcement and criminality in a society. How much these statistics are a self-perpetuating mental map in themselves is an interesting question. The city in which I now reside had been listed as one of the highest crime areas in the country. The police department, however, announced to general shock and relief that its computer had been incorrectly tabulating incidents of violent crime; they in fact numbered one seventh of the original figure reported. The city was transformed overnight, then, from Tombstone to Middletown.

5. But the 1960s were a time of unrest and social upheaval throughout the United States. With inner-city rioting, college campus rebellions against U.S. involvement in

Vietnam, civil rights protests, a rising crime rate, and the assassinations of prominent public figures John F. Kennedy, Malcolm X, Martin Luther King, Jr., and Robert Kennedy, public anxiety reached a pinnacle. Fear of crime rose as a topic of concern among U.S. residents and as a topic of research (Garafalo & Laub, 1978, p. 242; Gunter, 1994, p. 165).

6. This account of police behavior, based on participant observation, shows the patrolman to be the antithesis of a rule-bound bureaucrat. Van Maanen (1978c) depicts the street cop as increasingly isolated from both his or her supervisors and the community due to mobile patrols, rotating shifts, growing specialization within police departments, and increasingly well-defined subcultures in the society at large. This gives the street cop room to perform policing as he or she sees fit. Street police have more autonomy and discretion, but at the level of formal articulation, street cops in the literature of the time purport a loss of both. This loss, whether perceived or actual, has continued to be part of the street cops' perspective on contemporary policing.

7. See other works on how older people view the "decline" of their neighborhood and the lack of support of society (Anderson, 1990; Reider, 1985).

8. Unsurprisingly, a high number of those who assault police officers are intoxicated (Jager, 1983; Meyer, Megedanz, Chapman, Dahlin, & Swanson, 1981; Wright, 1990).

Real Cops and Mediated Cops
Can They "Get Along"?

Reviewers of past research on the content of prime-time cop shows, surveys of cop attitudes toward mass media, and the findings in this ethnography will note a contradiction. On one hand, it is clear that cops are as immersed in a mass-mediated culture as the rest of us: They are aware of their commodification in portrayals and specifically recite the stereotypes of mass-mediated cops. Drawing from their personal experiences, they can dismiss parts of the mass-mediated representation of police work and criminality as unrepresentative, even fantastic, or at least misleading: at worst an insidious demolition of their autonomy and authority, at best a glamorizing agent. As stated earlier, among the primary hoary myths that they assume are perpetuated (if not originated) on the screen are that (a) cops can dispense justice and keep the peace at will, even breaking the law—with few consequences—to do so; (b) cops can bring closure to criminality: they always "get their man" and solve the crime; (c) cops resolve cases quickly; and (d) cops' work lives consist of much action and violence. In turn, these beliefs compete with the street officer's attempts to control his own environment and negotiate his status with the public. In particular, the value they put on the experience of "being there" in some ways is undermined by the camera's ability to display events before the lens as if we the audience were actual witnesses of a dioramic and contextual reality. In a sense, the street cop must struggle with an invisible but omnipresent mediated cop for the attention and understanding of the citizenry that both—the former in reality, the latter in imitation of reality—are sworn to "protect and serve." Cops, an independent breed who chafe at being micromanaged, feel that mass media inconveniently pressure their public speech and behavior.

On the other hand, these sensibilities and observations are not systematic and produce no general theory of media influence on public behavior toward cops. For example, cops will with one breath dispute the TV stereotype but in another express beliefs that reflect or reify it. In public, they feel the need somewhat to play their own role in accordance with audience expectations; their disappointment when they fail to do so is evident. In private, they seem to wish that their own lives were more like those of the cops on TV: more action, less paperwork, greater respect from the public, cases that are resolved more easily and quickly, and so on. Finally, in seeking out pictures of themselves, they do not reject the stereotypes they identify; rather, they want to see themselves and encourage others to see them in heroic poses and action-packed behaviors.

Such being the case, it might be tempting to classify the cops' attitudes toward their own representation on mass media as unthoughtful and hypocritical. They make a third-person assumption of media's nefarious influences on others but fail to see how they themselves are acculturated to mediated values and stereotypes and, in their thoughts, words, and deeds, conform them to others. Such a conclusion, however, would itself be shallow. Mediated cops are in some of the aspects unreal (they do things no cop or human being could do) and inreal, that is, they do things that can occur in the daily life of real cops but do so on TV with much greater frequency and with an emphasis on kinesis and abbreviation of time (cf. Perlmutter, 1995, 1999). This latter quality is worthy of extensive study: Just how intensified is the reality of the mediated cop? Research suggests an amazing discordance between the street and screen in raw numbers of chases, shootings, and the like. Yet, the mediated cop is presented within codes of realism that, for most of us, render a perception of pseudo-authority on what cop work is "really like": As previously stated, the fantastic defines the vicarious. Cops know this; they are, after all, the real experts. But beyond knowing this, they also know that no magic wand or social movement will change the situation.

In addition, cops understand that they critique mass-mediated representations of themselves but also live among them. We all do, the ethnographer included. They and I, though in slightly different ways, feel the weight of TV and cinema. The pictures I took and the feelings I experienced in the squad car were both directly and indirectly influenced by mass media. Hence the utility of the metaphor of the "stream" and "mainstream" employed by Gerbner and his colleagues. We all live in the media stream; we can be very conscious of the force of the pressure; we can even find shallows and obstructions that temper its currents, yet it continues all encompassing and inexorable. Being aware of it does not make us free but rather, as it does for cops and it did for me, makes the struggles plainer. The purpose of this chapter is to try to resolve the seeming contradiction that awareness is not liberation.

PERCEPTIONS AS EFFECTS

There is evidence from a series of studies—unfortunately, none recently conducted—that cops may overestimate the power of TV to *directly* shape the public's view of them (Brooks & Friedrich, 1970; Dominick, 1974; Rarick, Townsend, & Boyd, 1973). The findings suggest that children and adolescents form their attitudes and perceptions of police and police behavior based on their perception of the attitudes of friends and family members. Actual contact with police and one's race also has some influence on perceptions and attitudes toward police. Crime show viewing is more influential on viewers' knowledge of such concepts as civil rights and efficacy of police than it is on viewers' attitudes toward police in general. Do such mechanisms, if they are still operative today, belie the perceptions of cops? Are they fashioning TV into a cause of the mean world rather than a symptom? To make such distinctions would be simplistic. Personal encounters, family prejudices, and peer group pressures are obviously important influences on human thought and behavior. But the indirect influences on extramedia reality are much harder to measure: How much do media influence or augment the spiral of expectation that in turn exacts interpersonal influence?

Moreover, cops behave as if what they do matters—suspicious of TV, they have not ceded the street to mediated realities. One of the ideas that has recurred frequently in this study is the premium that cops put in their direct language and in their metaphors and analogies on "thereness." It is worth reiterating now. Police officers are "there" at the scenes of crimes in progress and those already committed. In St. Louis Park (SLP), they are also there, typically before paramedics, in 911 medical emergencies. But the importance of thereness is also related to who is not there and the context of the subsequent machinations of the legal system. When the cops get there—as, for example, in the case of a woman who has been assaulted in her apartment after a break-in—there is usually no one else to witness what the cops see. They observe the rising bruises on the woman's eyes, jaw, and mouth and the rents in her clothing; they hear the agony in her voice and absorb her despair and fear. For someone like myself, who had only encountered such horrors through mediated imagery, the sight of the "real thing" is wrenching; for cops, it is routine. Later, of course, others become involved: A detective conducts the follow-up investigation, hospital staff perform an examination, and a social worker is called in for counseling. The "suits"—the lawyers—enter the picture. The cop will write up his narrative, and, to a large extent, the case passes out of his purveyance. A long time, perhaps years later, he may be asked to testify about what he saw in that first encounter. But he believes, with considerable validity, that the primary interaction cannot really be re-created, either by his own written narrative or by any dramatization, even by the documentary photographer or reality cop show videographer. Thus, cops may see media reality as a complication and intrusion: another irritant added to the ever-growing list.

This said, the valorizing, validating, and valuing of thereness can be read as a form of ego gratification. Certainly, members of any profession will claim a level of expertise, of inner knowledge, that outsiders have no access to or can only approximate. Cops, however, could contend that the reality of crime is their provenance, shared only with the victim and the criminal. I argue that this is one source of police resentment of their televisual portrayal. Cop shows purport to convey realism as if reality were possible to transmit on a 25-inch screen and in two dimensions, with commercial breaks. The acute aspects of the cops' work—the jolting, terror-filled moments, as well as the chronic routines of patrolling and form filing—find representations and analogs in media but not true real-time, multisensual re-creations. Elie Abel (1981) has written,

> Reality does not come neatly packaged in 2- or 3-minute lengths; raw history is filled with perversities, contradictions, ragged edges . . . [but] TV is a storytelling medium. It abhors ambiguities, ragged edges, and unresolved issues. . . . The effect all too frequently is to impose upon an event or situation a preconceived form that alters reality, heightening one aspect at the expense of another for the sake of a more compelling story, blocking out complications that get in the way of the narrative. (p. 68)

Being there endows cops with an authentic voice; television, in their view, robs them of the proprietary right, the stakeholders' claim, over that lived experience by providing a facsimile of it free to anyone who switches a dial. In this sense, the TV cop is the hustling, boastful competitor of the real-life street cop for public attention, sympathy, and respect.

This resentment, although often not expressed directly, would not be socially important if it were not based on the assumption, also held by cops, that the public—including taxpayers who vote on appropriations, victims of crime, and criminals—is deeply influenced by mass media representations of law enforcement and criminality. The mechanisms for such influence are unarticulated in detail. Cops are not social scientists concerned with the minutiae of whether, for example, TV acculturates or works through mimicry, imitation, desensitization, or any other mechanism. Basically, they think, TV leads people to presume things. A cop put it this way to me: *PP:* "They don't get to know me; they spend 5 minutes with me. But they spend 5 years with Sipowicz and Buntz." One of the elements of cop work that I was struck with in the ethnography was how time constraints, among other factors, rarely allowed police-public interactions to cover any more than the business at hand. Whatever one thinks of community policing, it is certainly true that cops rarely accord time for, nor is the public interested in, any meaningful mutual acquaintance. I think the police officers with whom I dealt would reject such sensitive social worker lingo, but they do maintain that people are largely unaware of some of the real challenges and limitations of their job.

What we can read from this is that perceptions matter. In a philosophic conversation I had with an officer, he related to me his theory of what a more formal scholar might call punctuated realism. He described a situation in the abstract, in which a man takes hostages at a supermarket. He holds a gun to the head of a woman clerk. The cops arrive, and the negotiations begin. The man is "wacko": He claims that the CIA, the Zionists, Dan Quayle, and humanoids from Alpha Centauri are conspiring to control his brain. The officer with whom I was speaking then begged the question, "So I'm negotiating with him. What should I say?" He asserted that he would not argue with the guy about his beliefs, no matter how patently false or substantially insane they were: "What's the point?" Instead, he would agree with him, ask questions, express interest, and then point out how the hostage taking would not expose the conspiracy but rather silence his important revelation that the world awaited with bated breath. Unlike a social worker or a psychologist, however, the cop added with a grin, once the man was disarmed and in handcuffs, the hostage safe, he (the cop) would tell the prisoner what a "fucking psycho" he was. In short, the policeman was expressing a functional theory of relativism that called for acceptance of a contradictory belief to achieve his goal. Once the goal was achieved, tolerance for the absurd or dangerous would be ceased immediately. Cops know, then, that to some extent, their work is a game of perceptions, gauging their own and purposely manipulating others'. Another source of cops' resentment of the perceived power of TV is that it bypasses the practice of their own street psychology.

The reason for this sense of competition is simple and drawn from the nature of police work and our understanding of the role of social drama in everyday life. As Turner, Goffman, and others have suggested, acting on stage is not an activity limited to certain cultural realms of expression and physical locations in society. All people are concerned, at one point or another, with impression management. Their public rituals and comportment, even their attire, may be calculated to play to certain audiences. In the back stage, other rituals and transcripts may emerge. The ethnographic literature abounds with such examples. Guy Oakes (1990), in his study of insurance company salesmen, found them torn between the contradictory edicts—both pushed by their companies—to be super profit makers but also to be "service" people. Robert A. Stebbins (1990) found a similar tension of oppositions in the world of stand-up comics: the back-stage sweating of details of the acts, rehearsal, and preparation, and the front stage of appearing "spontaneous." Acting, thus, is not the opposite state to being.

But police work is one of the few professions in which the public role is legally sanctioned to be *lethally* different from the private role. Cops have the power, as Bittner (1970) puts it, to justify "the exercise of provoked force required to meet illegitimate acts" (p. 36). When dressed in the navy blue uniform, a cop must act like a cop, capable of but circumspect about using deadly force, holding the life of others, including his own, in the balance. Apropos, one officer told me a brief anecdote of how, although his policy was to avoid telling others he was a policeman when off duty, he once "lost it" and brandished his occupation. Kept waiting for 2 hours in the dentist's office and later finding himself charged for a procedure he was never given, he blew up at the dentist, exclaiming, "I risk my life for 20 dollars an hour. What the hell do you do?" In fact, he mentioned this because it was an anomaly. Cops are perfectly willing to risk their lives for $20 an hour; in some parts of the country, they earn much less. But in return, they want to be treated by the public, their superiors, and the system itself in a manner that they, not some Hollywood actor, negotiate. Autonomy is the essential issue.

An obvious research question, which became part of my ethnography, is on what basis are the natives judging their performance? By standards that they feel they experience on the street, that is, personally experienced by themselves or peers? Or are those standards of accomplishment definitions of success and thus validation arising from outside of the physical universe in which they work and reside? As one researcher has put it, "The 'violence' in 'television violence' cannot be isolated, from its perpetrators, from its victims, from its positions within 'codes of conduct in action' " (Sparks, 1992, p. 119). It would be crudely deterministic to put this in a direct effects mode, to say that real cops feel depressed if they do not live up to the norms of Clint Eastwood in the Dirty Harry series, Jack Lord's McGarret, or the Andy Renko character on *Hill Street Blues*. If, at the end of a street scene, a car stop, or a suspicious incident, a cop does not "nail a crook," "book 'em," or "collar a perp," has he failed? These issues are much more complex and subtle than simply modeling or antimodeling of certain television characters. Rather, the cops themselves have evidence that their reference reality intermingles with the mediated reality of law enforcement and crime to the extent that it is less a case of one text imposing its standards on another than that the texts of the street and of television influence people's perceptions of each separate reality. Cops thus are unconvinced that television is truth; rather, they tend to operate as if others, especially the public, believe this to be so.

This perception, as well as all its corollaries and patterns of assumption and inference, is an important social phenomenon. It is tempting for researchers to divide perception and reality; to some extent, both cops and myself have done so for the purpose of analyzing and extrapolating on the differences between street reality and mediated reality. Yet it is obvious and inevitable that perceptions are powerful when people act on them as if they were fact. Social science and interpretive content-based research have not yet answered, nor will they likely ever do so satisfactorily, what are the affective and cognitive effects of mass media portrayals of law enforcement and criminality. That cops believe that these effects exist, however, influences what they do and say on the street. This is the strong suggestion, produced by participant observation and listening to the natives, of this ethnography. Criminologists or sociologists or even political reformers who wish to effect change in modes and results of policing must take the perception of media power into account. No social prescriptions that deny the role of media in everyday life or fail to understand the processes of indirect absorption of media norms will find any success. To understand real cops, we must view and talk to them but also look at and understand what they are seeing and talking about, including what they see on TV.

Such findings produced by an ethnography should of course not be considered definitive. Studies of beliefs about and absorbed norms of mass media in everyday life can take place in innumerable settings. Within the vast realm of law enforcement and criminality, the mass-mediated ethnography can examine other groups, locales, institutions, and teams. The already rich field of research on criminals and those who engage in acts defined by society as deviant, which eventually bring them into collision with police, can be in turn enriched by considering and seeking out opinions of and influences by mass media. Ethnographies similar to this one also can be conducted of different kinds of teams within the legal system. These may include purposive examinations of women officers or those from differing class or race backgrounds, issues largely untouched in this ethnography because of the relative gender and ethnic uniformity of the police department studied. For example, to what extent do women officers who, it is suggested, have a less confrontational style of people and image management on the street, reflect and deal with public and media-driven perceptions of their status (see Carson, 1993)? Is there an interplay with historical opposition among male police officers to women engaging in street patrols (Hunt, 1990)? The same question may be asked about officers of African American heritage. Do they see the stereotype of the black criminal as derived from mass media confirming or colliding with street experience and public perception, including that of the black public, of their role as police officers?[1] Another line of ethnographic investigation may be on the perceived (decoded) mixed messages of television, an issue not fully explored here. Are media such as TV viewed as primary colors, depicting a universal view of the "cop," or are there levels of gradation? Such research would be supplemented by more contextual content analyses. What of modal effects: Are all media (TV, print, cinema) or genres of representation (news, entertainment, "infotainment") conceived of as equally or differentially guilty or influential on similar or divergent imagery and ideas?[2] Finally, what of media use by the natives? No officer in my study described his watching of TV cop shows as "heavy," but this topic could be related to issues of selective exposure in assessing public reactions to mass media.[3]

THE STRUGGLE CONTINUES

The policeman as hero is a powerful and common theme in fictive and reality-based media, in film, and in television shows that portray law enforcement activities. But positive portrayals do not necessarily have positive social implications if social reality is in discordance with expectation. In being heroes who solve problems in mass media representations, real-life police officers may not come off as successful when compared to this standard. In this way, we could say that the police demonstration is distorted by being overly positive; real-world statistics show that police are not nearly as effective as their crime drama portrayals

Figure 7.1.

suggest. Restrictions of time and authority rarely accord police officers the kind of positive interaction that allows people to see them not just as "model minorities in blue" or as automatons of the state but also as human beings.

And of course we need cops to be there. In the very first ride-along I took with SLP police officers, we responded to a multicar accident. One child was killed, another injured. In the picture in Figure 7.1, an officer holds a third child while the paramedics and firefighters try to rescue and resuscitate the rest of the family. The incident yielded two rolls of pictures: some action, some gore. This is the most calm. It is an illustration of a simple way that cops can do good without kicking down a door or arresting a bank robber in progress. It is also one reflection of the many roles we expect from the men and women in uniform: savior, confessor, projection of our dissatisfaction with the system, donut chomper, brute, sympathetic hero, and exemplar of mass mediation. In photographing cops, I learned that the process of photography, of measuring a subject through a viewfinder, framing the borders of an image, and choosing when to depress the shutter were not isolates from the culture and the norms and forms of television, photojournalism, and film. Likewise, cops understand that they are performers in a manner analogous to their counterparts on prime time. The variety of the performance is almost inexhaustible, and it is difficult to imagine how any single actor could satisfy every audience (cf. Goldstein, 1979; Wilson, 1968). Cops may very well be damned if they do and damned if they don't, but in the end, whatever we project them to be, it is difficult to imagine how we could live without them.

Yet, a last question remains if we accept the premise that the public wants cops to play a prescribed role that the officers feel the system does not allow: Do we want this contradiction resolved? Do we want the truth to be revealed? Cops are trapped between the myths of the profession (cop as savior) and the realities of the street (the inability to instantly enact closure). Living out what Ibsen called the "life-illusion" may be preferable for all involved. In my own experience, it was unclear, as much as I valued spending time with officers, whether I was fully capable of or interested in being there at all times and in all circumstances. There were occasions when I pulled back, not wanting to completely share the adventures of my subjects. One moment in particular occurred on an early morning in February. It was cold, Minnesota cold, 30 to 40 degrees below zero with wind chill, hard-packed snow on the ground. By all rights it should have been a dead night, but there was a call. A man had been at a party, had gotten into an argument with his wife, and stalked out into the night. He had not returned to the party, not taken the car, and not shown up at home. The worry was that he had become disoriented and had collapsed and now was somewhere in the woods or on someone's lawn dying of hypothermia.

We drove around looking for the man and eventually came to an old railway bridge. It was the only nonstreet route that would connect the line of sight between the location of the party and the man's home. It was part of the job that we should go over the bridge and take a look. We got out of the car; I took my camera but never used it. For the first time in my police experience I was terrified. The timbers of the bridge were about a foot apart, with only open space between them, and a frozen stream lay what seemed a hundred yards below. Of course, the timbers were iced over. For about a third of the way over the bridge I trudged behind the officer, measuring my steps as carefully as a soldier in an unmarked minefield. After my third or fourth near slip, I gave up. I told the cop, whom I considered a friend, "I can't do it. I'm going back to the car." He nodded. There was no attribution of guilt or recrimination, at least registered in his face. He turned around and continued onwards.

I tottered back to the police car. The cop was gone about 15 minutes, which worried me because I was still thawing from my arrested bridge experience. Finally he returned and dropped himself with a thud into the driver's seat. There were no icicles dangling from his nose, but he was almost blue with cold. Yet he managed a smile and said, "I should've gone back with you." He didn't tell me about the conditions after I gave up; he didn't have to. We called in that we had not found the man; 2 hours later his wife phoned the police station to say that he had been asleep in an unsearched room in the house the entire time. The officer and I both laughed when we heard the dispatcher release this information; you really had to be there.

My aborted participation with the natives at this juncture was predicated on a reasonable calculation of my own fear and a measure of my lack of coordination. But I think it is another analogy to the public view of police work. Cops, as well as Hollywood producers, would probably agree that a truly realistic portrayal of police officers would be greeted with stupefaction and indifference by the mass audience. Likewise, cops understand that the yearning people have for common sense, justice, and preservation of peace is not purely an artifact of television. Our desire to have a hero sanction our aggrievement, solve our problems, and make our lives better with a wave of a baton or a gold shield is ancient and universal. The tradition of using force to achieve justice is equally ancient and common. Hammurabi, the Babylonian king, proclaimed that he was ordained by the gods "to promote the welfare of the people" and in his law code wished "To cause justice to prevail in the country/To destroy the wicked and evil,/That the strong may not oppress the weak" (Roux, 1980, p. 189). Indeed, the Old Testament is replete with a spirit of *Lex talionis*—where God or his anointed ones are the swords of retaliation for crimes and great sins. Alfred the Great, the popular early medieval king of England, was praised for his laws but also for his *personal* intercession in the name of law: "Injure ye not the widows and step-children, nor hurt them anywhere; for if ye do otherwise, they will cry unto me, and I will hear them, and I will then slay you with my sword; and I will do so that your wives be widows, and your children will be step-children" (Thorpe, 1840, p. 53). In medieval society, every man played the policing function for his neighbors, responsible for his "kin" under the biblical injunction to be "my brother's keeper" (Reith, 1956). It is difficult to read these admonishments and not think of them as more formal or florid versions of the unspoken motto of the mass-mediated cop and the expectations held of the real one.

Thus, the legitimate question can be raised: Do people really want the curtain pulled back? Do we want to know what cops are really like, or would we prefer that they more uniformly live up to the stereotype? Stereotypes, after all, are not necessarily only prejudices and misapprehensions of the world but also hopes and anticipations of that world. Shattering the mediated reality of cops may, in this sense, do greater damage to the justice system, whatever remains of it, than perpetuating the stereotypes. Society is no longer willing to give cops the relatively unlimited power they had or perceived that they had in the "good old days," but we want them to solve problems as if that power still existed. This is a contradiction in the body politic as well as the mind of the street cop.

Cops live the opposition between what they must pretend to be and what the system actually lets them be, between the performance the public wants—even though the public is often contradictory and desultory about what it wants exactly—and the performance that it is in them to give. Such tensions are of course strong in many other kinds of work in which people must be "on" in public, that is, perform roles to get messages across and succeed in their vocation. This is a *struggle,* the word Marx defined as the meaning of life, and the continuation of the struggle signifies for cops taking seriously their oath to protect and serve. Everyone in a community has the right to debate what rules of engagement and comportment should govern the cop's attempt to enforce the law and keep the peace, but in the end, the voice of cops must be listened to because being there really is radically different from watching it on TV or even riding along a couple of times.

And this all matters very much because cops matter. As seen, street cops are correct in their own assessment of the job's importance: They are the gatekeepers, and in many ways their initial actions determine when some event is categorized as crime, who is accused, and even to what extent the perpetrator is punished (Sheley & Nock, 1979). Making cops happier, more satisfied with their work, and more comfortable in their roles are all desirable goals—for cops and for us. There are limits on what can be done, of course: Many are moral and constitutional. As a character in Orson Welles's *Touch of Evil* notes, "A policeman's job is only easy in a police state." I do not think that cops want or would be happy serving the latter. Yet, asking cops what they want, observing them, and letting them speak openly all may help create a better community. This is not an easy task, as evidenced by the paucity and contradictory nature of research on police job satisfaction (Dhillon, 1990; Lefkowitz, 1974; Sheley & Nock, 1979; see also Regoli, Crank, & Culbertson, 1989). Perhaps a first step to helping cops is a simple one: We can begin to make the cops' struggle less onerous when we admit we really know very little about them.

Struggle, however, fails to describe how much of the cops' negotiations for and performances of status, identity, and control are resolved or at least alleviated by their own equanimity. They would rebel at being portrayed as aggrieved victims. They are sanctioned by society to be stars in the street theater of crime and law enforcement, but many of the situations in which they find themselves and the characters they confront ring more like farce than tragedy. Indeed, they sometimes appear to be more *compère* than dramatic hero. In my time with the SLP cops, I never found them any more or less sarcastic about their "clients" than were the clerks at a video store I worked at for 6 months.[4] Griping, feeling undervalued, and ascribing stupidity and dishonesty to the customers are universals of human work practice. In this vein, cops, no more and no less than school teachers or bank clerks, do not want sympathy and would feel quite uncomfortable at some sort of larger public movement to clean up their television image and extend greater understanding for their real-life dilemmas. This attitude was crystallized for me by one officer who, after a good 5 minutes of detailing the main irritations and complaints of the police, chuckled as an emergency call crackled over the radio and he went to lights and sirens: "Hey, don't get me wrong. I love this job. Let's go!"

NOTES

1. This would be interesting in light of the mixed messages of TV content. In dramatic series of the early 1970s, Dominick (1973) found that whites are overrepresented as perpetrators of crime. Estep and Macdonald (1983) found that prime-time television crime drama portrayed murder suspects as predominantly white, middle-class, middle-aged males, far different from the typical suspect recorded in police statistics: young, lower-class male, disproportionately black. In contrast, in news and information and reality-based entertainment programming, black perpetrators are overrepresented, at least in terms of frequency of portrayals associated with crimes (Entman, 1990; Oliver, 1994; Sheley & Ashkins, 1981).

2. A study by Stroman and Seltzer (1985) examined the impact of media in the formation of public opinion about crime. The researchers determined subjects' perceptions of the causes of crime vis-à-vis which medium, print or television, each subject reported using the most as a source of news. Those reporting that they used predominantly newspapers as their source of news perceived poverty to be the main cause of crime, but those reporting that they used mostly television as their news source targeted a lenient court system as the reason people committed crimes. Those using television most were more likely to view environmental and societal ills as the primary cause of crime than were subjects relying on radio.

3. Testing the relationship between arousal and enjoyment, Wakshlag et al. (1983) found that crime drama is especially alarming for persons already apprehensive about victimization. Exposure to an experimental message such as a crime drama with a disturbing ending caused decreased enjoyment and increased distress in these already fearful viewers.

4. I found Ph.D. students to be much more insulting and ridiculing of professors than the cops were of their superiors and their "customers." Now that I am a professor, the way that my colleagues and I talk about our students would, if made public through some recording device by an enterprising reporter for the school paper, elicit fury from our pupils, their parents, and the administration alike.

Appendix

Table A.1 List of Network Prime-Time Crime and Law Enforcement Programs by Year, 1947–1994

1947	None
1948	None
1949	
The Black Robe	30 minutes
Famous Jury Trials	30 minutes
Look Photocrime	30 minutes
Man Against Crime	30 minutes
Martin Kane, Private Eye	30 minutes
1950	
Adventures of Ellery Queen	30 minutes
Dick Tracy	30 minutes
Famous Jury Trials	30 minutes
Inside Detective	30 minutes
Man Against Crime	30 minutes
Martin Kane, Private Eye	30 minutes
The Plainclothesman	30 minutes
They Stand Accused	60 minutes
Treasury Men in Action	30 minutes
1951	
Adventures of Ellery Queen	30 minutes
Amazing Mr. Malone/Mr. District Attorney	30 minutes
Charlie Wild, Private Detective	30 minutes
Crime Syndicated	30 minutes
Crime With Father	30 minutes
Man Against Crime	30 minutes
Martin Kane, Private Eye	30 minutes
The Plainclothesman	30 minutes
Racket Squad	30 minutes
Rocky King, Detective	30 minutes
They Stand Accused	60 minutes
Treasury Men in Action	30 minutes

1952
  Adventures of Ellery Queen   30 minutes
  Crime Syndicated   30 minutes
  Dragnet/Gangbusters   30 minutes
  Inspector Mark Saber   30 minutes
  Man Against Crime   30 minutes
  Martin Kane, Private Eye   30 minutes
  The Plainclothesman   30 minutes
  Racket Squad   30 minutes
  Rocky King, Detective   30 minutes
  Steve Randall   30 minutes
  They Stand Accused   60 minutes
  Treasury Men in Action   30 minutes
1953
  Dragnet   30 minutes
  Inspector Mark Saber   30 minutes
  Man Against Crime   30 minutes
  Martin Kane, Private Eye   30 minutes
  The Plainclothesman   30 minutes
  Rocky King, Detective   30 minutes
  Treasury Men in Action   30 minutes
1954
  Dragnet   30 minutes
  Justice   30 minutes
  The Lineup   30 minutes
  Public Defender   30 minutes
  Rocky King, Detective   30 minutes
  The Stranger   30 minutes
  They Stand Accused   60 minutes
  Treasury Men in Action   30 minutes
1955
  Dragnet   30 minutes
  Justice   30 minutes
  The Lineup   30 minutes
  Wanted   30 minutes
1956
  Dragnet   30 minutes
  The Lineup   30 minutes
1957
  Court of Last Resort   30 minutes
  Dragnet   30 minutes
  The Lineup   30 minutes
  M Squad   30 minutes
  Meet McGraw   30 minutes
  Perry Mason   60 minutes
  Saber of London   30 minutes
  Thin Man   30 minutes
1958
  Adventures of Ellery Queen   60 minutes
  Confession   30 minutes
  Dragnet   30 minutes
  The Lineup   30 minutes
  M Squad   30 minutes
  Naked City   30 minutes

Perry Mason	60 minutes
Peter Gunn	30 minutes
Saber of London	30 minutes
77 Sunset Strip	60 minutes
Thin Man	30 minutes
Traffic Court	30 minutes
1959	
Bourbon Street Beat	60 minutes
Court of Last Resort	30 minutes
Hawaiian Eye	60 minutes
Hennessey	30 minutes
Lawless Years	30 minutes
The Lineup	60 minutes
M Squad	30 minutes
Markham	30 minutes
Perry Mason	60 minutes
Peter Gunn	30 minutes
Philip Marlowe	30 minutes
Richard Diamond, Private Detective	30 minutes
Robert Taylor: The Detectives	30 minutes
77 Sunset Strip	60 minutes
Staccato	30 minutes
Tightrope	30 minutes
The Untouchables	60 minutes
1960	
Andy Griffith Show	30 minutes
Bourbon Street Beat	60 minutes
Dan Raven	60 minutes
Harrigan and Son	30 minutes
Hawaiian Eye	60 minutes
Hennessey	30 minutes
The Law and Mr. Jones	30 minutes
Michael Shayne	60 minutes
Naked City	60 minutes
Perry Mason	60 minutes
Peter Gunn	30 minutes
Robert Taylor: The Detectives	30 minutes
77 Sunset Strip	60 minutes
Surfside Six	60 minutes
The Untouchables	60 minutes
The Witness	60 minutes
1961	
Andy Griffith Show	30 minutes
Cain's Hundred	60 minutes
Car 54, Where Are You?	30 minutes
Checkmate	60 minutes
The Defenders	60 minutes
87th Precinct	60 minutes
Hawaiian Eye	60 minutes
Hennessey	30 minutes
The Investigators	60 minutes
Naked City	60 minutes
The New Breed	60 minutes
Perry Mason	60 minutes

Robert Taylor's Detectives	60 minutes
77 Sunset Strip	60 minutes
Surfside Six	60 minutes
The Untouchables	60 minutes

1962

Andy Griffith Show	30 minutes
Car 54, Where Are You?	30 minutes
The Defenders	60 minutes
Hawaiian Eye	60 minutes
Naked City	60 minutes
Perry Mason	60 minutes
77 Sunset Strip	60 minutes
The Untouchables	60 minutes

1963

Andy Griffith Show	30 minutes
Arrest and Trial	90 minutes
Burke's Law	60 minutes
The Defenders	60 minutes
The Fugitive	60 minutes
Perry Mason	60 minutes
77 Sunset Strip	60 minutes

1964

Andy Griffith Show	30 minutes
Burke's Law	60 minutes
The Defenders	60 minutes
The Fugitive	60 minutes
Perry Mason	60 minutes

1965

Amos Burke, Secret Agent	60 minutes
Andy Griffith Show	30 minutes
The F.B.I.	60 minutes
The Fugitive	60 minutes
Perry Mason	60 minutes
Trials of O'Brien	60 minutes

1966

Andy Griffith Show	30 minutes
The F.B.I.	60 minutes
Felony Squad	30 minutes
The Fugitive	60 minutes
Hawk	60 minutes

1967

Andy Griffith Show	30 minutes
Dragnet	30 minutes
The F.B.I.	60 minutes
Felony Squad	30 minutes
Ironside	60 minutes
Judd, for the Defense	60 minutes
Mannix	60 minutes
N.Y.P.D.	30 minutes

1968

Adam 12	30 minutes
Dragnet	30 minutes
The F.B.I.	60 minutes
Felony Squad	30 minutes
Hawaii Five-O	60 minutes

Ironside	60 minutes
It Takes a Thief	60 minutes
Judd, for the Defense	60 minutes
Mannix	60 minutes
Mayberry R.F.D.	30 minutes
Mod Squad	60 minutes
N.Y.P.D.	30 minutes
The Outsider	60 minutes

1969

Adam 12	30 minutes
Bold Ones: The Lawyers/The Protectors	60 minutes
Dragnet	30 minutes
The F.B.I.	60 minutes
Hawaii Five-O	60 minutes
Ironside	60 minutes
It Takes a Thief	60 minutes
Mannix	60 minutes
Mayberry R.F.D.	30 minutes
Mod Squad	60 minutes

1970

Adam 12	30 minutes
Bold Ones: The Lawyers/The Senator	60 minutes
Dan August	60 minutes
The F.B.I.	60 minutes
Hawaii Five-O	60 minutes
Ironside	60 minutes
Mannix	60 minutes
Mayberry R.F.D.	30 minutes
Mod Squad	60 minutes
The Most Deadly Game	60 minutes
Silent Force	30 minutes
Storefront Lawyers	60 minutes
Young Lawyers	60 minutes

1971

Adam 12	30 minutes
Bold Ones: The Lawyers	60 minutes
Cade's County	60 minutes
Cannon	60 minutes
The D.A.	30 minutes
The F.B.I.	60 minutes
Hawaii Five-O	60 minutes
Ironside	60 minutes
Longstreet	60 minutes
Mannix	60 minutes
Mod Squad	60 minutes
NBC Mystery Movie:	90 minutes
Columbo/McCloud/McMillan and Wife	
O'Hara, U.S. Treasury	60 minutes
Owen Marshall	60 minutes
The Partners	30 minutes
The Persuaders	60 minutes

1972

Adam 12	30 minutes
Banyon	60 minutes
Cannon	60 minutes

The F.B.I.	60 minutes
Hawaii Five-O	60 minutes
Ironside	60 minutes
Mannix	60 minutes
Mod Squad	60 minutes
NBC Sunday Mystery Movie:	90 minutes
Columbo/McCloud/McMillan and Wife/Hec Ramsey	
NBC Wednesday Mystery Movie:	90 minutes
Madigan/Cool Million/Banacek	
Owen Marshall	60 minutes
The Rookies	60 minutes
Streets of San Francisco	60 minutes

1973

Adam 12	30 minutes
Barnaby Jones	60 minutes
Cannon	60 minutes
Chase	60 minutes
The F.B.I.	60 minutes
Griff	60 minutes
Hawaii Five-O	60 minutes
Ironside	60 minutes
Kojak	60 minutes
Mannix	60 minutes
NBC Sunday Mystery Movie:	120 minutes
Columbo/McCloud/McMillan and Wife/Hec Ramsey	
NBC Wednesday Mystery Movie:	90 minutes
Madigan/Tenafly/Faraday & Company/The Snoop Sisters	
New Adventures of Perry Mason	60 minutes
Owen Marshall	60 minutes
Police Story	60 minutes
The Rookies	60 minutes
Streets of San Francisco	60 minutes
Toma	60 minutes
Tuesday Night CBS Movie: *Hawkins/Shaft*	90 minutes

1974

Adam 12	30 minutes
Barnaby Jones	60 minutes
Cannon	60 minutes
Get Christie Love	60 minutes
Harry-O	60 minutes
Hawaii Five-O	60 minutes
Ironside	60 minutes
Kodiak	30 minutes
Kojak	60 minutes
Manhunter	60 minutes
Mannix	60 minutes
Nakia	60 minutes
NBC Sunday Mystery Movie:	120 minutes
Columbo/McCloud/McMillan and Wife/Amy	
Prentiss	
Petrocelli	60 minutes
Police Story	60 minutes
Police Woman	60 minutes
Rockford Files	60 minutes

The Rookies	60 minutes
Streets of San Francisco	60 minutes
1975	
Baretta	60 minutes
Barnaby Jones	60 minutes
Barney Miller	30 minutes
Bronk	60 minutes
Cannon	60 minutes
Ellery Queen	60 minutes
Harry-O	60 minutes
Hawaii Five-O	60 minutes
Joe Forrester	60 minutes
Kate McShane	60 minutes
Kojak	60 minutes
Matt Helm	60 minutes
NBC Sunday Mystery Movie:	
Columbo/McCloud/McMillan and Wife/McCoy	120 minutes
Petrocelli	60 minutes
Police Story	60 minutes
Police Woman	60 minutes
Rockford Files	60 minutes
The Rookies	60 minutes
S.W.A.T.	60 minutes
Starsky & Hutch	60 minutes
Streets of San Francisco	60 minutes
Switch	60 minutes
1976	
Baretta	60 minutes
Barnaby Jones	60 minutes
Barney Miller	30 minutes
Blue Knight	60 minutes
Charlie's Angels	60 minutes
Delvecchio	60 minutes
Hawaii Five-O	60 minutes
Kojak	60 minutes
Most Wanted	60 minutes
NBC Sunday Mystery Movie:	90 minutes
Columbo/McCloud/McMillan/Quincy, M.E.	
Police Story	60 minutes
Police Woman	60 minutes
The Practice	30 minutes
Rockford Files	60 minutes
Serpico	60 minutes
Starsky and Hutch	60 minutes
Streets of San Francisco	60 minutes
Switch	60 minutes
1977	
Baretta	60 minutes
Barnaby Jones	60 minutes
Barney Miller	30 minutes
Carter Country	30 minutes
Charlie's Angels	60 minutes
CHiPs	60 minutes
Hardy Boys Mysteries/Nancy Drew Mysteries	60 minutes

Hawaii Five-O	60 minutes
Kojak	60 minutes
Police Woman	60 minutes
Quincy, M.E.	60 minutes
Rockford Files	60 minutes
Rosetti and Ryan	60 minutes
Starsky and Hutch	60 minutes
Switch	60 minutes

1978

Barnaby Jones	60 minutes
Barney Miller	30 minutes
Carter Country	30 minutes
Charlie's Angels	60 minutes
CHiPs	60 minutes
Eddie Capra Mysteries	60 minutes
Hardy Boys Mysteries	60 minutes
Hawaii Five-O	60 minutes
Kaz	60 minutes
Quincy, M.E.	60 minutes
Rockford Files	60 minutes
Starsky and Hutch	60 minutes
Vega$	60 minutes

1979

The Associates	30 minutes
Barnaby Jones	60 minutes
Barney Miller	30 minutes
Big Shamus, Little Shamus	60 minutes
Charlie's Angels	60 minutes
CHiPs	60 minutes
Detective School	30 minutes
Eischied	60 minutes
Hart to Hart	60 minutes
Hawaii Five-O	60 minutes
Kate Loves a Mystery	60 minutes
Misadventures of Sheriff Lobo	60 minutes
Paris	60 minutes
Quincy, M.E.	60 minutes
Rockford Files	60 minutes
Vega$	60 minutes

1980

Barney Miller	30 minutes
Charlie's Angels	60 minutes
CHiPs	60 minutes
Enos	60 minutes
Freebie and the Bean	60 minutes
Hart to Hart	60 minutes
Hill Street Blues	60 minutes
Lobo	60 minutes
Magnum, P.I.	60 minutes
Quincy, M.E.	60 minutes
Vega$	60 minutes
Walking Tall	60 minutes

1981
  Barney Miller   30 minutes
  CHiPs   60 minutes
  Hart to Hart   60 minutes
  Hill Street Blues   60 minutes
  Magnum, P.I.   60 minutes
  McClain's Law   60 minutes
  Quincy, M.E.   60 minutes
  Shannon   60 minutes
  Simon & Simon   60 minutes
  Strike Force   60 minutes
  Today's F.B.I.   60 minutes
1982
  Cagney & Lacey   60 minutes
  CHiPs   60 minutes
  Devlin Connection   60 minutes
  Hart to Hart   60 minutes
  Hill Street Blues   60 minutes
  Magnum, P.I.   60 minutes
  Matt Houston   60 minutes
  Quincy, M.E.   60 minutes
  Remington Steele   60 minutes
  Simon & Simon   60 minutes
  T. J. Hooker   60 minutes
  Tucker's Witch   60 minutes
1983
  Hardcastle & McCormick   60 minutes
  Hart to Hart   60 minutes
  Hill Street Blues   60 minutes
  Magnum, P.I.   60 minutes
  Matt Houston   60 minutes
  The Mississippi   60 minutes
  Remington Steele   60 minutes
  Simon & Simon   60 minutes
  T. J. Hooker   60 minutes
1984
  Cagney & Lacey   60 minutes
  Hardcastle & McCormick   60 minutes
  Hawaiian Heat   60 minutes
  Hill Street Blues   60 minutes
  Hot Pursuit   60 minutes
  Hunter   60 minutes
  Jessie   60 minutes
  Magnum, P.I.   60 minutes
  Matt Houston   60 minutes
  Miami Vice   60 minutes
  Mickey Spillane's Mike Hammer   60 minutes
  Murder, She Wrote   60 minutes
  Night Court   30 minutes
  Partners in Crime   60 minutes
  Remington Steele   60 minutes
  Riptide   60 minutes

Simon & Simon	60 minutes
T. J. Hooker	60 minutes
1985	
Cagney & Lacey	60 minutes
Crazy Like a Fox	60 minutes
The Equalizer	60 minutes
Hardcastle & McCormick	60 minutes
Hill Street Blues	60 minutes
Hollywood Beat	60 minutes
Hunter	60 minutes
Lady Blue	60 minutes
Lime Street	60 minutes
Magnum, P.I.	60 minutes
Miami Vice	60 minutes
Moonlighting	60 minutes
Murder, She Wrote	60 minutes
Night Court	30 minutes
Our Family Honor	60 minutes
Remington Steele	60 minutes
Riptide	60 minutes
Simon & Simon	60 minutes
Spenser: For Hire	60 minutes
1986	
Cagney & Lacey	60 minutes
Crime Story	60 minutes
Downtown	60 minutes
The Equalizer	60 minutes
Heart of the City	60 minutes
Hill Street Blues	60 minutes
Hunter	60 minutes
L.A. Law	60 minutes
Magnum, P.I.	60 minutes
Matlock	60 minutes
Miami Vice	60 minutes
Moonlighting	60 minutes
Murder, She Wrote	60 minutes
New Mike Hammer	60 minutes
Night Court	30 minutes
Simon & Simon	60 minutes
Sledge Hammer	30 minutes
Spenser: For Hire	60 minutes
1987	
Cagney & Lacey	60 minutes
Crime Story	60 minutes
The Equalizer	60 minutes
Hooperman	30 minutes
Houston Knights	60 minutes
Hunter	60 minutes
J. J. Starbuck	60 minutes
Jake and the Fatman	60 minutes
L.A. Law	60 minutes
The Law and Harry McGraw	60 minutes

Leg Work	60 minutes
Magnum, P.I.	60 minutes
Matlock	60 minutes
Miami Vice	60 minutes
Moonlighting	60 minutes
Murder, She Wrote	60 minutes
Night Court	30 minutes
Ohara	60 minutes
The Oldest Rookie	60 minutes
Private Eye	60 minutes
Sledge Hammer	30 minutes
Spenser: For Hire	60 minutes
21 Jump Street	60 minutes
Wiseguy	60 minutes

1988

America's Most Wanted	30 minutes
The Equalizer	60 minutes
Hooperman	30 minutes
Hunter	60 minutes
In the Heat of the Night	60 minutes
Knightwatch	60 minutes
L.A. Law	60 minutes
Matlock	60 minutes
Miami Vice	60 minutes
Moonlighting	60 minutes
Murder, She Wrote	60 minutes
Murphy's Law	60 minutes
Night Court	30 minutes
Police Story	120 minutes
Simon and Simon	60 minutes
Sonny Spoon	60 minutes
21 Jump Street	60 minutes
Wiseguy	60 minutes

1989

ABC Saturday Mystery:	120 minutes
B. L. Stryker/Columbo/Kojak/Christine Cromwell	
America's Most Wanted	30 minutes
Booker	60 minutes
Cops	30 minutes
Hunter	60 minutes
In the Heat of the Night	60 minutes
Jake and the Fatman	60 minutes
L.A. Law	60 minutes
Mancuso, FBI	60 minutes
Matlock	60 minutes
Murder, She Wrote	60 minutes
Night Court	30 minutes
Snoops	60 minutes
21 Jump Street	60 minutes
Wiseguy	60 minutes
Wolf	60 minutes

1990
  Against the Law   60 minutes
  America's Most Wanted   60 minutes
  Cop Rock   60 minutes
  Cops   30 minutes
  D.E.A.   60 minutes
  Father Dowling Mysteries   60 minutes
  Gabriel's Fire   60 minutes
  Hunter   60 minutes
  In the Heat of the Night   60 minutes
  Jake and the Fatman   60 minutes
  L.A. Law   60 minutes
  Law & Order   60 minutes
  Matlock   60 minutes
  Murder, She Wrote   60 minutes
  Night Court   30 minutes
  Top Cops   30 minutes
  Trials of Rosie O'Neill   60 minutes
1991
  America's Most Wanted   60 minutes
  American Detective   30 minutes
  The Antagonists   60 minutes
  The Commish   60 minutes
  Cops   60 minutes
  FBI: The Untold Stories   30 minutes
  I'll Fly Away   60 minutes
  In the Heat of the Night   60 minutes
  Jake and the Fatman   60 minutes
  L.A. Law   60 minutes
  Law & Order   60 minutes
  Murder, She Wrote   60 minutes
  Night Court   30 minutes
  Pacific Station   30 minutes
  Palace Guard   60 minutes
  Pros and Cons   60 minutes
  Reasonable Doubts   60 minutes
  Top Cops   60 minutes
  Trials of Rosie O'Neill   60 minutes
1992
  America's Most Wanted   60 minutes
  Angel Street   60 minutes
  Civil Wars   60 minutes
  The Commish   60 minutes
  Cops   60 minutes
  Hat Squad   60 minutes
  I'll Fly Away   60 minutes
  In the Heat of the Night   60 minutes
  L.A. Law   60 minutes
  Law & Order   60 minutes
  Likely Suspects   30 minutes
  Murder, She Wrote   60 minutes

Picket Fences	60 minutes
Reasonable Doubts	60 minutes
The Round Table	60 minutes
Secret Service	60 minutes
Top Cops	60 minutes
1993	
America's Most Wanted	60 minutes
Bakersfield P.D.	30 minutes
The Commish	60 minutes
Cops	60 minutes
In the Heat of the Night	60 minutes
L.A. Law	60 minutes
Law & Order	60 minutes
Matlock	60 minutes
Missing Persons	60 minutes
Murder, She Wrote	60 minutes
NYPD Blue	60 minutes
Picket Fences	60 minutes
South of Sunset	60 minutes
Walker, Texas Ranger	60 minutes
1994	
America's Most Wanted	60 minutes
The Commish	60 minutes
Cops	60 minutes
The Cosby Mysteries	60 minutes
Diagnosis Murder	60 minutes
Due South	60 minutes
Homicide: Life on the Streets	60 minutes
Law & Order	60 minutes
Murder, She Wrote	60 minutes
NYPD Blue	60 minutes
New York Undercover	60 minutes
Picket Fences	60 minutes
Sweet Justice	60 minutes
Under Suspicion	60 minutes
Walker, Texas Ranger	60 minutes

SOURCE: Data drawn from Brooks and Marsh (1995)
NOTE: Program must feature some aspect of law, policing, or criminality.

Table A.2 Network Prime-Time Hours of Crime and Law Enforcement Programming, 1947–1994

Year	Hours in Prime Time Per Week
1947	0
1948	0
1949	2.5
1950	5
1951	6.5
1952	6.5
1953	4
1954	4.5
1955	2
1956	1
1957	4.5
1958	7.5
1959	11.5
1960	13
1961	14.5
1962	7
1963	7
1964	4.5
1965	5.5
1966	4
1967	6
1968	10.5
1969	8.5
1970	11.5
1971	15
1972	13.5
1973	20.5
1974	18.5
1975	22.5
1976	17.5
1977	14
1978	12
1979	14.5
1980	11.5
1981	10.5
1982	12
1983	9
1984	17.5
1985	18.5
1986	17
1987	22.5
1988	17.5
1989	15.5
1990	15.5
1991	17
1992	16.5
1993	13.5
1994	15

NOTE: Calculated from Table A.1.

Table A.3 Network Prime-Time Programs Whose Main or Lead Characters Include
Uniformed Patrol Officers

1947	None
1948	None
1949	None
1950	None
1951	None
1952	None
1953	
Man Behind the Badge	30 minutes
1954	None
1955	
Wanted	30 minutes
1956	None
1957	None
1958	None
1959	None
1960	None
1961	
Car 54, Where Are You?	30 minutes
1962	
Car 54, Where Are You?	30 minutes
1963	None
1964	None
1965	None
1966	None
1967	None
1968	
Adam 12	30 minutes
1969	
Adam 12	30 minutes
1970	
Adam 12	30 minutes
1971	
Adam 12	30 minutes
1972	
Adam 12	30 minutes
The Rookies	60 minutes
1973	
Adam 12	30 minutes
Police Story	60 minutes
The Rookies	60 minutes
1974	
Adam 12	30 minutes
Nakia	60 minutes
Police Story	60 minutes
The Rookies	60 minutes
1975	
Joe Forrester	60 minutes
Police Story	60 minutes
The Rookies	60 minutes
1976	
Blue Knight	60 minutes
Police Story	60 minutes

1977	
CHiPs	60 minutes
1978	
CHiPs	60 minutes
1979	
CHiPs	60 minutes
1980	
CHiPs	60 minutes
Hill Street Blues	60 minutes
1981	
CHiPs	60 minutes
Hill Street Blues	60 minutes
1982	
CHiPs	60 minutes
Hill Street Blues	60 minutes
T. J. Hooker	60 minutes
1983	
Hill Street Blues	60 minutes
T. J. Hooker	60 minutes
1984	
Hill Street Blues	60 minutes
T. J. Hooker	60 minutes
1985	
Hill Street Blues	60 minutes
Our Family Honor	60 minutes
1986	
Hill Street Blues	60 minutes
1987	None
1988	
Police Story	120 minutes
1989	
Cops	30 minutes
1990	
Cop Rock	60 minutes
Cops	30 minutes
Top Cops	30 minutes
1991	
Cops	60 minutes
Top Cops	30 minutes
1992	
Cops	60 minutes
Top Cops	30 minutes
1993	
Bakersfield P.D.	30 minutes
Cops	60 minutes
1994	
Cops	60 minutes

NOTE: Program must feature uniformed, regular, nonranking, patrol police officers as lead characters.

References

Abel, E. (1981). Television in international conflict. In A. Arno & W. Dissayanake (Eds.), *The news media and national and international conflict* (pp. 63-70). Boulder, CO: Westview.

Alicke, M. D., Braun, J. C., Glor, J. E., Kotiz, M. L., Magee, J., Sederholm, H., & Siegel, R. (1992). Complaining behavior in social interaction. *Personality and Social Psychology Bulletin, 18,* 286-295.

Alpert, G., & Anderson, P. (1986). The most deadly force: Police pursuits. *Justice Quarterly, 3,* 1-14.

Alpert, G., & Dunham, R. (1992). *Policing urban America* (2nd ed.). Prospect Heights, IL: Waveland.

Alpert, G., & Fridell, L. (1992). *Police vehicles and firearms: Instruments of deadly force.* Prospect Heights, IL: Waveland.

Anderson, E. (1990). *Streetwise: Race, class and change in an urban community.* Chicago: University of Chicago Press.

Arcuri, A. (1977). You can't take fingerprints off water: Police officers' views toward 'cop' television shows. *Human Relations, 30,* 237-247.

Bahn, C. (1984). Police socialization in the eighties: Psychological consequences of becoming a police officer. *Journal of Police Science and Administration, 10*(3), 347-348.

Barnouw, E. (1990). *Tube of plenty: The evolution of American television* (2nd ed.). New York: Oxford University Press.

Barrile, L. (1980). *Television and attitudes about Crime.* Unpublished doctoral dissertation, Department of Sociology, Boston College.

Bayley, D. H., & Bittner, E. (1993). Learning the skills of policing. In R. G. Dunham & G. P. Alpert (Eds.), *Critical issues in policing: Contemporary readings* (pp. 106-129). Prospect Heights, IL: Waveland.

Beauregard, R. A. (1993). Representing urban decline: Post war cities as narrative objects. *Urban Affairs Quarterly, 29*(4), 187-202.

Becker, H. (1963). *Outsiders: Studies in the sociology of deviance.* New York: Free Press.

Becker, H. (1974). Photography and sociology. *Studies in the Anthropology of Visual Communications, 1*(1), 3-26.

Becker, H. (1995). Visual sociology, documentary photography, and photojournalism: It's (almost) all a matter of context. *Visual Sociology, 10*(1-2), 5-14.

Bercal, T. (1970). Calls for police assistance. *American Behavioral Scientist, 13*, 681-691.

Bittner, E. (1967). The police on skid-row: A study of peace-keeping. *American Sociological Review, 32*, 699-715.

Bittner, E. (1970). *The functions of the police in modern society.* Rockville, MD: National Institute of Mental Health.

Black, D. (1970). Production of crime rates. *American Sociological Review, 35*, 733-748.

Black, D. J., & Reiss, A. J., Jr. (1970). Police control of juveniles. *American Sociological Review, 35*, 63-77.

Brooks, D., & Friedrich, G. (1970). Police image: An exploratory study. *Journal of Communication, 20*, 370-374.

Brooks, T., & Marsh, E. (1995). *The complete directory to prime time network and cable TV shows.* New York: Ballantine.

Carlson, J. (1983). Crime show viewing by pre-adults: The impact on attitudes toward civil liberties. *Communication Research, 10*(4), 529-552.

Carlson, J. (1985). *Prime time law enforcement: Crime show viewing and attitudes toward the criminal justice system.* New York: Praeger.

Carson, B. (1993). Women in law enforcement. In S. Macdonald, P. Holden, & S. Ardener (Eds.), *Images of women in peace and war* (pp. 67-80). Boulder, CO: Lynne Riener.

Caspi, A., Bem, D. J., & Elder, G. H., Jr. (1989). Continuities and consequences of interactional styles across the life course. *Journal of Personality, 57*, 375-406.

Cavender, G., & Bond-Maupin, L. (1993). Fear and loathing on reality television: An analysis of "America's Most Wanted" and "Unsolved Mysteries." *Sociological Inquiry, 63*(3), 305-317.

Chalfen, R. (1987). *Snapshot versions of life.* Bowling Green, OH: Bowling Green State University Press.

Chandler, R. (1988). *The simple art of murder.* New York: Vintage. (Original work published 1950)

Clark, R. (1972). *Delinquency.* New York: Hammer.

Cohen, J., & Davis, R. G. (1991). Third-person effects and the differential impact in negative political advertising. *Journalism Quarterly, 68*, 680-688.

Cohen, J., Mutz, D., Price V., & Gunther, A. (1988). Perceived impact of defamation: An experiment on third-person effects. *Public Opinion Quarterly, 52*, 161-173.

Collier, J., Jr., & Collier, M. (1986). *Visual anthropology: Photography as a research method* (Rev. ed.). Albuquerque: University of New Mexico Press.

Comrie, M., & Kings, E. (1975). *Study of urban workloads: Final report.* London: Home Office Police Research Services Unit.

Cordner, G., & Trojanowicz, R. (1992). Patrol. In G. Cordner & D. Hale (Eds.), *What works in policing? Operations and administration examined* (pp. 1-18). Cincinnati, OH: Anderson.

Coser, L. (1956). *Continuities in the study of social conflict.* New York: Free Press.

Cumming, E., Cumming, I., & Edell, L. (1965). Policeman as philosopher, guide and friend. *Social Problems, 12*, 276-286.

Davison, W. P. (1983). The third-person effect in communication. *Public Opinion Quarterly, 47*(1), 1-15.

DeFleur, L. (1975). Biasing influences on drug arrest records: Implications for deviance research. *American Sociological Review, 40,* 88-103.

Denyer, T., Callender, R., & Thompson, D. L. (1975). The policeman as alienated labor. *Journal of Police Science and Administration, 3,* 251-258.

Dershowitz, A. (1983). *The best defense.* New York: Vintage.

Dhillon, P. K. (1990). Some correlates of job satisfaction: A study of police personnel. *Psychological Studies, 35,* 197-204.

Dominick, J. (1973). Crime and law enforcement on T.V. *Public Opinion Quarterly, 37*(2), 241-250.

Dominick, J. (1974). Children's viewing of crime shows and attitudes on law enforcement. *Journalism Quarterly, 51*(1), 5-12.

Entman, R. (1990). Modern racism and the images of blacks in local television news. *Critical Studies in Mass Communication, 7,* 332-345.

Erickson, M., & Jenson, G. (1977). Delinquency is still group behavior. *Journal of Criminal Law and Criminology, 68,* 262-273.

Ericson, R. (1982). *Reproducing order: A study of police patrol work.* Toronto: University of Toronto Press.

Ericson, R. (1991). Mass media, crime, law, and justice. *British Journal of Criminology, 31*(3), 219-249.

Ericson, R. (1993). *Making crime: A study of detective work* (2nd ed.). Toronto: University of Toronto Press.

Ericson, R. (1994a). The division of expert knowledge in policing and security. *British Journal of Sociology, 45,* 149-175.

Ericson, R. (1994b). The Royal Commission on criminal justice system surveillance. In M. McConville & L. Bridges (Eds.), *Criminal justice in crisis* (pp. 113-140). Aldershot, UK: Edward Elgar.

Ericson, R., Baranek, P., & Chan, J. (1987). *Visualizing deviance: A study of news organization.* Toronto: University of Toronto Press.

Ericson, R., Baranek, P., & Chan, J. (1989). *Negotiating control: A study of news sources.* Toronto: University of Toronto Press.

Ericson, R., Baranek, P., & Chan, J. (1991). *Representing order: Crime, law and justice in the news media.* Toronto: University of Toronto Press.

Erikson, K. V., Cheatham, T. R., & Haggard, C. R. (1976). A survey of police communication training. *Communication Education, 25*(4), 299-306.

Estep, R., & Macdonald, P. (1983). How prime time crime evolved on TV (1976-1981). *Journalism Quarterly, 60,* 293-300.

Faccioli, P., & Harper, H. (1996). IVSA 96: Echos of Eco. *Visual Sociology, 11*(2), 3-7.

Festinger, L., Schachter, S., & Back, K. (1963). *Social pressures in informal groups: A study of human factors in housing.* Stanford, CA: Stanford University Press.

Fine, G. A. (1977). Popular culture and social interaction: Production, consumption, and usage. *Journal of Popular Culture, 11,* 453-466.

Fine, G. A. (1980). Cracking diamonds: Observer role in a little league baseball setting and the acquisition of social competence. In W. B. Shaffir, R. A. Stebbins, & A. Turowitz (Eds.), *Fieldwork experience* (pp. 117-132). New York: St. Martin's.

Fine, G. A. (1993). Ten lies of ethnography: The moral dilemmas of field research. *Journal of Contemporary Ethnography, 22*(3), 267-294.

Gamson, W., Crocteau, D., Hoynes, W., & Sasson, T. (1992). Media images and the social construction of reality. *Annual Review of Sociology, 18,* 373-393.

Garafalo, J., & Laub, J. (1978). The fear of crime: Broadening our perspective. *Victimology, 3*(3-4), 242-253.

Garland, D. (1996). The limits of the sovereign state. *British Journal of Criminology, 36*(4), 445-471.

Geertz, C. (1973). *The interpretation of cultures.* New York: Basic Books.

Gerbner, G. (1969). The television world of violence. In D. Lange, R. Baker, & S. Ball (Eds.), *Mass media and violence* (pp. 311-339). Washington, DC: Government Printing Office.

Gerbner, G. (1972). Violence in television drama: Trends and symbolic functions. In G. A. Comstock & E. A. Rubinstein (Eds.), *Television and social behavior: Media content and control* (Vol. 1, pp. 28-187). Rockville, MD: National Institute of Mental Health.

Gerbner, G. (1980). Trial by television: Are we at the point of no return? *Judicature, 63*(9), 416-426.

Gerbner, G., & Gross, L. (1980). The violent face of television and its lessons. In E. Palmer & A. Dorr (Eds.), *Children and the faces of television* (pp. 149-162). New York: Academic Press.

Gerbner, G., Gross, L., Morgan, M., & Signorielli, N. (1980). The mainstreaming of America: Violence profile 11. *Journal of Communication, 30,* 10-20.

Gerbner, G., Gross, L., Morgan, M., & Signorielli, N. (1982). Charting the mainstream: Television's contribution to political orientations. *Journal of Communication, 32,* 100-127.

Gerbner, G., Gross, L., Morgan, M., & Signorielli, N. (1994). Growing up with television: The cultivation perspective. In J. Bryant & D. Zillman (Eds.), *Media effects: Advances in theory and research* (pp. 17-41). Hillsdale, NJ: Lawrence Erlbaum.

Goffman, E. (1959). *The presentation of self in everyday life.* Garden City, NY: Doubleday.

Gold, S. (1991). Ethnic boundaries and ethnic entrepreneurs: A photo-elicitation study. *Visual Sociology, 6*(2), 9-22.

Goldstein, H. (1979). *Policing in a free society.* Cambridge, MA: Harvard University Press.

Grady, J. (1996). The scope of visual sociology. *Visual Sociology, 11*(2), 10-24.

Greenberg, B. (1980). *Life on television: Content analysis of U.S. TV drama.* Norwood, NJ: Ablex.

Greene, J. R. (1989). Police officer job satisfaction and community perceptions: Implications for community oriented policing. *Research in Crime and Delinquency, 26,* 168-183.

Griswold, W. (1994). *Cultures and societies in a changing world.* Thousand Oaks, CA: Pine Forge.

Gunter, B. (1994). The question of media violence. In J. Bryant & D. Zillman (Eds.), *Media effects: Advances in theory and research* (pp. 163-212). Hillsdale, NJ: Lawrence Erlbaum.

Gunther, A. C. (1991). What we think others think: Cause and consequences in the third-person effect. *Communication Research, 18,* 355-372.

Guttman, S. (1993, June 21). The breeding ground. *National Review, 54,* 47-55.

Hageman, M., Kennedy, R., & Price, N. (1981). Coping with stress. In H. More, (Ed.), *Critical issues in law enforcement* (pp. 281-288). Cincinnati, OH: Anderson.

Harper, H. (1987). *Working knowledge: Skill and community in a small shop.* Chicago: University of Chicago Press.

Harper, H. (1990). Visual sociology at the University of Amsterdam: Personal notes and reflections. *Visual Sociology, 5*(2), 34-40.

Harris, R. (1978). The police academy and the professional self-image. In P. K. Manning & J. Van Maanen (Eds.), *Policing: A view from the street* (pp. 273-291). Santa Monica, CA: Goodyear.

Head, S. (1954). Content analysis of television drama programs. *Quarterly of Film, Radio and Television, 9,* 175-194.

Herr, M. (1973). *Dispatches.* New York: Random House.

Hindelang, M., Hirschi, T., & Weis, J. (1981). *Measuring delinquency.* Newbury Park, CA: Sage.

Hirst, P. (1994). *Associative democracy: New forms of social and economic governance.* Cambridge, UK: Polity.

Hunt, J. (1990). The logic of sexism among police. *Women and Criminal Justice, 1,* 3-30.

Jager, J. (1983). Assaults on German police officers. *Police Studies, 6,* 18-21.

Jeanjean, M. (1990). *Un Ethnologie Chez les Policiers.* Paris: Editions Anne-Marie M,taill,.

Jorgensen, B. (1981). Transferring trouble: The initiation of reactive policing. *Canadian Journal of Criminology, 23,* 257-278.

Jowett, G. (1976). *Film: The democratic art.* Boston: Focal.

Kasinitz, P., & Hillyard, D. (1995). The old-timer's tale: The politics of nostalgia on the waterfront. *Journal of Contemporary Ethnography, 24*(2), 139-164.

Katz, J. (1987). What makes crime "news?" *Media, Culture and Society, 9,* 47-75.

Kelling, G., Pate, T., Dieckman, D., & Brown, C. (1974). *The Kansas City preventive patrol experiment: A summary report.* Washington, DC: Police Foundation.

Kinsey, R. (1985). *Merseyside crime and police surveys: Final report.* Liverpool, UK: Merseyside County Council.

Klockars, C. (1980). The Dirty Harry problem. *Annals of the American Academy of Political and Social Science, 33,* 452.

Kowalski, R. M. (1996). Complaints and complaining: Functions, antecedents, and consequences. *Psychological Bulletin, 119,* 179-196.

Lash, S., & Urry, J. (1987). *The end of organized capitalism.* Cambridge, UK: Polity.

Lefebvre, G. (1973). *The great fear of 1789.* New York: Schocken.

Lefkowitz, J. (1974). Job attitudes of police: Overall description and demographic correlates. *Journal of Vocational Behavior, 5,* 221-230.

Lester, D. (Ed.). (1979). *A search for correlates of job satisfaction in police officers.* Cincinnati, OH: Academy of Criminal Justice Sciences.

Lester, D. (1987). Correlates of job satisfaction in police officers. *Psychological Reports, 60,* 550.

Lichter, L., & Lichter, R. (1983). *Prime time crime.* Washington, DC: Media Institute.

Linton, J. M. (1992). Documentary film research's unrealized potential in the communication field. *Communication, 13,* 85-93.

Loeber, R., & Stouthamer-Loeber, M. (1986). Family factors as correlates and predictors of juvenile conduct problems and delinquency. In M. Tonry & N. Morris (Eds.), *Crime and justice: An annual review* (Vol. 7, pp. 29-149). Chicago: University of Chicago Press.

Manning, P. K. (1977). *Police work: The social organization of policing.* Cambridge: MIT Press.

Manning, P. K. (1986). Rules, colleagues, and situationally justified actions. In P. K. Manning & J. Van Maanen (Eds.), *Policing: A view from the street* (pp. 71-90). Santa Monica, CA: Goodyear.

Manning, P. K. (1988). *Symbolic communication: Signifying calls and the police response.* Cambridge: MIT Press.

Meehan, A. (1993). Internal police records and the control of juveniles: Politics and policing in a suburban town. *British Journal of Criminology, 33,* 504-524.

Meyer, C. K., Megedanz, T. C., Chapman, S. G., Dahlin, D. C., & Swanson, C. (1981). A comparative assessment of assault incidents: Robbery-related ambush, and general police assaults. *Journal of Police Science and Administration, 10,* 1-18.

National Television Violence Study, Volume 1. (1997). Thousand Oaks, CA: Sage.

Nelson, G. (1985). The findings of the national viewers' survey. In G. Barlow & A. Hill (Eds.), *Video violence and children* (pp. 33-53). New York: St. Martin's.

Nielsen Report. (1995). Report on television. New York: Nielsen Media Research.

Oakes, G. (1990). *The soul of the salesman: The moral ethos of personal sales.* New York: Humanitas.

O'Hara, C. E., & O'Hara, G. E. L. (1994). *Fundamentals of criminal investigation* (6th ed.). Springfield, IL: Charles C Thomas.

O'Hara, R. (1961). *Media for the millions: The process of mass communication.* New York: Random House.

Oliver, M. (1994). Portrayals of crime, race, and aggression in "reality based" police shows: A content analysis. *Journal of Broadcasting & Electronic Media, 38*(2), 179-192.

Ouellet, L. J. (1990). *Pedal to the metal: The work lives of truckers.* Philadelphia, PA: Temple University Press.

Parks, R. (1982). *The western hero in film and television: Mass media mythology.* Ann Arbor, MI: UMI Research Press.

Percy, S., & Scott, E. (1985). *Demand processing and performance in public service agencies.* University: University of Alabama Press.

Perlmutter, D. D. (1992). The vision of war in high school social science textbooks. *Communication, 13,* 143-160.

Perlmutter, D. D. (1994). Visual historical methods: Problems, prospects, applications. *Historical Methods, 27*(4), 167-184.

Perlmutter, D. D. (1995). Opening up photojournalism. *Visual Communication Quarterly, 2*(2), 9-11.

Perlmutter, D. D. (1997). Manufacturing visions of society and history in social science textbooks. *Journal of Communication, 47*(3), 1-14.

Perlmutter, D. D. (1998). *Photojournalism and foreign policy: Framing icons of outrage in international crises.* Westport, CT: Greenwood.

Perlmutter, D. D. (1999). *Visions of war: Picturing warfare from the Stone Age to the cyber age.* New York: St. Martin's.

Police Foundation. (1977). *Domestic violence and the police: Studies in Detroit and San Francisco.* Washington, DC: Author.

Police Studies Institute. (1983). *Police and people in London: Vol. 3. A survey of police officers.* London: Author.

Punch, M. (1979). *Policing the inner city.* London: Macmillan.

Punch, M. (1985). *Conduct unbecoming: The social construction of police deviance and control.* London: Tavistock.

Punch, M. (1986). *The politics and ethics of fieldwork.* Beverly Hills, CA: Sage.

Radelet, L. A., & Carter, D. L. (1994). *The police and the community.* New York: Macmillan.

Rarick, D., Townsend, J., & Boyd, D. (1973). Adolescent perceptions of police: Actual and as depicted in TV drama. *Journalism Quarterly, 50,* 438-446.

Ray, R. (1985). *A certain tendency of the Hollywood cinema, 1930-1980.* Princeton, NJ: Princeton University Press.

Redl, F. (1942). Group emotion and leadership. *Psychiatry, 5,* 573-596.

Regoli, R. M., Crank, J. P., & Culbertson, R. G. (1989). Police cynicism, job satisfaction, and work relations of police chiefs: An assessment of the influence of department size. *Sociological Focus, 22,* 161-171.

Regoli, R. M., Poole, E. D., & Hewitt, J. D. (1979). Exploring the empirical relation between police cynicism and work alienation. *Journal of Police Science and Administration, 7,* 336-339.

Reider, J. (1985). *Canarsie: The Jews and Italians of Brooklyn against liberalism.* Cambridge, MA: Harvard University Press.

Reiner, R. (1992). *The politics of the police* (2nd ed.). Toronto: University of Toronto Press.

Reith, C. (1956). *A new study of police history.* Edinburgh, UK: University of Edinburgh Press.

Riley, D., & Shaw, M. (1985). *Parental supervision and juvenile delinquency.* London: HMSO.

Roux, G. (1980). *Ancient Iraq* (2nd ed.). London: Penguin.

Rubenstein, J. (1973). *City police.* New York: Farrar, Straus, and Giroux.

Rubenstein, J. (1978). Controlling people. In P. K. Manning & J. Van Maanen (Eds.), *Policing: A view from the street* (pp. 255-265). Santa Monica, CA: Goodyear.

Sacks, H. (1972). Notes on police assessment of moral character. In D. Sudnow (Ed.), *Studies in social interaction* (pp. 280-293). New York: Free Press.

Sampson, R., & Laub, J. (1993). *Crime in the making.* Cambridge, MA: Harvard University Press.

Schlesinger P., & Tumber, H. (1994). *Reporting crime: The media politics of criminal justice.* Oxford, UK: Oxford University Press.

Schwartz, D. (1992). *Waucoma twilight.* Washington, DC: Smithsonian.

Scott, J. C. (1990). *Domination and the arts of resistance: Hidden transcripts.* New Haven, CT: Yale University Press.

Secord, P. F., & Backman, C. W. (1964). *Social psychology.* New York: McGraw-Hill.

Selye, H. (1956). *The stress of life.* New York: McGraw-Hill.

Shadgett, P. (1990). *An observational study of police patrol work.* Unpublished master's thesis, Center of Criminology, University of Toronto.

Shearing, C. (1984). *Dial-a-cop: A study of police mobilization.* Toronto: Centre of Criminology, University of Toronto.

Shearing, C., & Ericson, R. (1991). Culture as figurative action. *British Journal of Sociology, 42,* 481-506.

Sheley, J., & Ashkins, C. (1981). Crime, crime news, and crime views. *Public Opinion Quarterly, 19,* 321-325.

Sheley, J. F., & Nock, S. L. (1979). Determinants of police job satisfaction. *Sociological Inquiry, 49,* 49-55.

Sherif, M., & Cantril, H. (1947). *The psychology of ego involvements.* New York: John Wiley.

Shils, E. (1950). Primary groups in the American army. In R. K. Merton & P. Lazersfeld (Eds.), *Continuities in social research: The studies in the scope and method of the American soldier* (pp. 16-39). New York: Free Press.

Simmel, G. (1955). *Conflict & the web of group-affiliations* (K. H. Wolff & R. Bendix, Trans.). New York: Free Press.

Singletary, M. W., & Stull, G. (1980). Evaluation of media by Pennsylvania police chiefs. *Journalism Quarterly, 57*(4), 655-658.

Sklar, R. (1975). *Movie-made America: A cultural history of American movies.* New York: Vintage.

Slovak, J. S. (1978). Work satisfaction and municipal police officers. *Journal of Police Science and Administration, 6,* 462-470.

Smith, G., & Gray, J. (1983). *Police and people in London: Vol. 4. The police in action.* London: Policy Studies Institute.

Smythe, D. (1954). Reality as presented by TV. *Public Opinion Quarterly, 18,* 143-156.

Sparks, R. (1992). *Television and the drama of crime: Moral tales and the place of crime in public life.* Buckingham, UK: Open University Press.

Stebbins, R. A. (1990). *The laugh-makers: Stand-up comedy as art business, and lifestyle.* Montreal: McGill-Queen's University Press.

Stewert, D., & Sullivan, T. (1982). Illness behavior and the sick role in chronic disease: The case of multiple sclerosis. *Social Science and Medicine, 16,* 1397-1404.

Stroman, C. A., & Seltzer, R. (1985). Media use and perceptions of crime. *Journalism Quarterly, 62*(2), 340-345.

Subcommittee on the Constitution and the Subcommittee on Juvenile Justice of the Committee on the Judiciary United States Senate. (1990). Washington, DC.

Sykes, R. E. (1975). A theory of deference exchange in police-civilian encounters. *American Journal of Sociology, 81,* 587-600.

Tannen, D. (1998). *The argument culture: Moving from debate to dialogue.* New York: Random House.

Thorpe, B. (1840). *Ancient laws and institutes of England* (Vol. 1). London: Eyre & Spotiswoode.

Thucydides. (1928). *History of the Peloponnesian War* (Books 1-2, C. F. Smith, Ed. & Trans.). Cambridge, MA: Harvard University Press.

Trujillo, N., & Dionisopoulos, G. (1987). Cop talk, police stories, and the social construction of organizational drama. *Central States Speech Journal, 38*(3-4), 196-209.

Turner, P. (1987). *History of photography.* New York: Exeter.

Turner, V. (1982). *From ritual to theater: The human seriousness of play.* New York: Performing Arts Journal Publications.

Turner, V. (1986). *The anthropology of performance.* New York: Performing Arts Journal Publications.

Turner, W. (1968). *The police establishment.* New York: Putnam.

U.S. Department of Justice Statistics, Office of Justice Programs. (1997). *Police use of force: Collection of national data.* Washington, DC: Author.

Van Maanen, J. (1978a). Epilogue on watching the watchers. In P. K. Manning & J. Van Maanen (Eds.), *Policing: A view from the street* (pp. 309-349). Santa Monica, CA: Goodyear.

Van Maanen, J. (1978b). Observations in the making of policemen. In P. K. Manning & J. Van Maanen (Eds.), *Policing: A view from the street* (pp. 292-308). Santa Monica, CA: Goodyear.

Van Maanen, J. (1978c). The asshole. In P. K. Manning & J. Van Maanen (Eds.), *Policing: A view from the street* (pp. 221-254). Santa Monica, CA: Goodyear.

Wakshlag, J., Bart, L., Dudley, J., Grotrh, G., McCutcheon, J., & Rolla, C. (1983). Viewer apprehension about victimization and crime drama programs. *Communication Research, 10*(2), 195-217.

Walsh, W. (1986). Patrol officer arrest rates: A study of the social organization of police work. *Justice Quarterly, 2,* 271-290.

Webster, J. (1970). Police task and time study. *Journal of Criminal Law, Criminology and Police Science, 61,* 94-100.

Whyte, W. H. (1943). *Street corner society.* Chicago: University of Chicago Press.

Wilson, J. Q. (1968). *Varieties of police behavior.* Cambridge, MA: Harvard University Press.

Wirth, L. (1945). The problem of minority groups. In R. Linton (Ed.), *The science of man in the world crisis* (pp. 347-372). New York: Columbia University Press.

Wright, J. N. (1990). *A study of assaults on South Australian police officers.* Adelaide: South Australian Police Department.

Wright, R. (1978). *Six-guns and society.* Boulder, CO: Westview.

Wynnejones, P. (1985). Educationalists' report. In G. Barlow & A. Hill (Eds.), *Video violence and children* (pp. 141-159). New York: St. Martin's.

Index

About the Author

David D. Perlmutter teaches political communication at Louisiana State University's Manship School of Mass Communication in Baton Rouge. He is author of *Photojournalism and Foreign Policy* (1998), *Visions of War* (1999), and editor of the *Manship School Guide to Political Communication* (1999).